THE FIFER

of San Jacinto

BY LEE McGIFFIN

Illustrated by Frank Nicholas

LOTHROP, LEE AND SHEPARD CO., INC.

New York

With Thanks to
RICHARD, ROGER,
DON, GAVIN, AND RICH

Contents

The Fifer of San Jacinto

CHAPTER ONE

The Promised Land

The lone white-topped wagon came to a lurching halt, and Page Carter loosened the reins wrapped around his aching wrists. He clenched his fists to hide the blisters on his hands, and looked across the river where smoke from hidden chimneys curled above the moss-hung oak trees.

"There it is, Mom, Serena on the Brazos—the River of the Arms of God."

The slender, weary-faced woman beside him on the high wagon seat straightened her black cambric bonnet. "Yes," she said quietly, "It's Texas, the Promised Land. I only wish—"

They sat silent, then. Page knew what she was thinking. It had been his father, Jefferson Carter, who had wanted to come to Texas. Jefferson Carter, the schoolmaster at the Academy in Richmond, Virginia, who had been so sure Texas was the Promised Land.

Page remembered the letters his father received from his old friend, Benton Fairfax, who had gone to the frontier three years ago. Mr. Fairfax said Texas was a wonderful country. He had a prosperous cotton plantation. There were no schools, and a man with very little money could have his own academy in no time. Land was cheap and the cotton was tall.

There had been long talks between his parents. Jefferson Carter could never hope to own an academy in Richmond. He would go on being just a hired schoolmaster. But in Texas! His own academy!

Then came the decision that shattered the pleasant little world Page had known. They were going to Texas.

He hadn't wanted to leave the little red brick house with his small room high up under the eaves. He liked walking down the cobbled street to the big white academy. He liked the games after school, liked racing his little black mare, Charcoal, on Saturdays, and the quietness of the steepled church on Sundays. But Jefferson Carter had promised Page he could come back in a few years to attend the University of Virginia. With that to count on, it was easier when they sold the house and joined an immigrant train to the West.

For a boy of fifteen who never before had been away from Richmond, the journey became a lark and an adventure as the wagon wheels rolled pleasantly through

Georgia, Alabama, and Mississippi. Sleeping in the open, seeing new country, and making new friends, Page almost forgot how much he hated leaving Virginia.

He danced with the others when a fiddle sang around the campfire at night. He listened to his father play "Come to the Bower" on his silver flute. And when the wagon train laid over a day in a small village, he raced Charcoal against all comers and won.

Then came the driving rains against the wagon tops in Louisiana. His father, never an outdoors man, fell ill with a fever and Page drove the cumbersome wagon through heavy mud to the next settlement.

There they had left Jefferson Carter in a country graveyard. Page remembered how his pen knife had scratched the fresh pine board as he carved the date— "April 4, 1835."

There was nothing to do but go on with the wagon train. After they had crossed into Texas, the other settlers, one by one, turned off, leaving the Carter wagon to travel a lonely trail to the bank of the Brazos.

"We'd best decide what to do, Mom." As he looked at the river, Page tried to sound as dependable and wise as his father always had. "I know Mr. Fairfax meant us to stay with him on the plantation until Father could get the academy started but now—"

Mrs. Carter looked up at the awkward, long-boned boy whose voice had trailed off so uncertainly. His dark

hair had need of cutting. His face was white and strained with worry.

"What do you think we should do?"

Page began to feel more confident. "We could sell the horses and wagon and take passage back by boat. Steamboats come up the Brazos this far. Back in Virginia I could earn a living for us, Mom."

Susan Carter looked down at the blanket of bluebonnets stretching to the ferry and listened to the stillness of the woods. "You may be right, Page, but let's ask Mr. Fairfax first. There comes the ferry across for us. Drive on down the bank."

Page looked back into the wagon at the four-poster bed, the loom and spinning wheel, the churn, the boxes of china and silver, the rosewood desk, the books, the kitchen safe with its dwindling supply of coffee, meal, sugar and beans. He leaned over and tucked his father's flute and fife into the round-topped trunk. He wondered if he could ever get such a load across on the log ferry.

Slapping the horses with his reins, he braked the wagon down the bank, and hoped the red-faced ferryman didn't know he had never driven a team onto a raft.

But the ferryman had apparently seen newcomers before. He led the horses aboard with yelling, slapping and general heave-ho and saw that Charcoal was tied securely to the wagon wheel. He looked up at the anxious faces.

"Don't you worry none, ma'am. This here ferry ain't

about to sink. I carried heavier loads than this! Where you folks from?"

"Richmond, Virginia," Page answered.

"Fixing to stop in Serena?"

"For tonight, yes." Page had often heard his father keep his own counsel with strangers. He decided to do the same.

The man had untied the ferry now and picked up his long pole. Pushing off the bank, he steered and poled into the muddy red water.

Realizing the man knew his business, Page looked up and down the Brazos. Downstream he could see the skip and dash of the water as it ran over rocks. Upstream, the river flowed majestically, banked by heavy timber and grassy meadowland.

It seemed to him they were standing still in midstream, until he was suddenly aware of the west bank looming in front of them. "Here you are," the ferryman called as he nosed the raft to its mooring tree. "Safe and sound like I told you. Take you back and forth any time you say, excepting high waters. Flood time, don't nobody cross the Brazos. That will be, let's see—three animals, wagon, two people—a dollar and two bits."

Page gave him the money and shouted to the horses. Slowly they strained up the steep rise to the road above. Then the creaking of the wagon was still. This was Serena.

The late afternoon sun shadowed the dusty road that

stretched for a half mile to the north and south. On either side among the giant live oaks were scattered crude log cabins with clay chimneys. Dogs slept placidly in the wagon tracks. A pig scuttled across the road. A high-wheeled cart lumbered behind patient oxen.

Page didn't know what he had expected, but disappointment settled on him like a blanket. He slumped over the reins, trying not to show what his face could not hide.

He looked at his mother and saw the disappointment in her eyes. Quickly he pulled himself tall in the wagon seat. "Let's go to the inn for the night and drive out to the plantation tomorrow."

Susan Carter smoothed her dark skirt as though she were driving down the main street of Richmond on a Sunday afternoon. "Yes, Page. We'll put up for the night. It will be good to sleep in a real bed again."

Page drove on. The first cabin was a blacksmith shop where he could see a stocky man shoeing a horse. The man waved as they went by. They passed a general store with several wagons tied outside. The next place was apparently a saloon, judging from the noise. A few more cabins were set well back in the woods, and then came the wagon yard.

People waved, children called from doorways, but there was no inn. Grimly, Page turned the wagon and went back toward the ferry. "I'll ask the blacksmith the way to the Fairfax plantation. We can make it there tonight."

He stopped in front of the smithy, handed the reins to his mother and climbed over the front wheel. He could see the square, ruddy face of the man above the heat of the forge. He noticed the blackened buckskin britches and the hard muscled bare arms that rose and fell with the big hammer.

He waited until the smith had finished the shoe. "I beg your pardon sir, but could you direct me to the Fairfax plantation?"

The blacksmith dropped his hammer on the hard packed dirt floor. "Fairfax? Benton Fairfax? Who are you, boy?"

"I'm Page Carter, sir. My mother and I just drove in. We are expected at the Fairfax plantation."

The smith glanced outside at Susan Carter sitting quietly on the wagon seat. "Send your pa in. I'd have a word with him."

Page fought down a mounting weariness. "My father died in Louisiana. I drove my mother on. There's no inn here so we had best go on to the plantation. It's been a long trip, sir."

The big man with the calloused hands drew Page to the back of the shop. "Right sorry about your pa. Guess I might as well tell you. There aren't any Fairfaxes. And there's no plantation."

"But my father had letters from him, asking him to come and start an academy, to teach school!"

"Look son, I'm Marker Wilson. I knew Benton was figuring on bringing a schoolmaster here. We need one bad. But—well, I don't know how to say this except straight out. The whole Fairfax family got wiped out by Indians a month ago. Burned down the house and run off the stock, took the slaves, and ruint the cotton crop."

Page felt as though he had been hit in the face.

"Here, sit down, boy. I know this is a right bitter thing to happen. Your mother will take it hard, so you best think what to tell her. Women get frightened easy. Truth is, been no Indians around here for two years. Kind of surprised us this time. Feel better now, son?"

Page wiped his sweaty face on his cotton shirt sleeve. "Yes, sir. Thank you. I'll tell my mother."

Marker Wilson scowled into the gathering dusk. "Go easy on womenfolks, son."

Page knew the big man was trying to soften the blow. "My mother is not one to weep, Mr. Wilson. We'll sleep in the wagon and make our plans tomorrow. My father had the deed to a lot in Serena. If you could tell me where it is, we could stay there. It would be quieter than the wagon yard."

"Wagon yard is no place for a lady. Get me that deed, and we'll find the lot you own."

Page went to the wagon and rummaged in the trunk. "Mr. Wilson wants to see our lot deed, Mom."

The blacksmith looked at the paper. "Light's poor here. Read off the number to me."

Page took the paper. "It's block three, lot nine, sir."

The smith scratched his shaggy head, pulled at his ear, and then sized up the boy as though trying to guess his weight and strength. "Getting nigh unto good dark out there now. You just tell your ma, gentle like, about the Fairfax folks and then both of you stay the night here. We'll find your lot come morning."

Page had a strange feeling that something about the deed was not right. But he was bone-weary, and beat down with a load of worry he was not used to carrying.

As he climbed back on the wagon, Susan Carter asked quietly. "What happened to Benton Fairfax?"

"They were all killed by Comanches a month ago," he said.

Before she could speak, Marker Wilson put his hand on the wheel. "Mrs. Carter, ma'am, I'm sorry for your trouble. You must be mighty near tired out. My cabin isn't much, but I would take it kindly should you stay the night. The boy and I can bed down in the wagon back of the shop."

Susan Carter lifted her head and managed to smile at the man in the dirty buckskins. "Thank you, Mr. Wilson. I am fair in need of some rest." She stepped over the wagon wheel and Marker Wilson put her carefully on the ground.

"Hand me my apron from the trunk, Page. I'll wager Mr. Wilson is just as hungry as you are."

CHAPTER TWO

Redheaded Stranger

When Page opened his eyes to the grey light of morning he couldn't remember where he was. Then it all came back as he heard the heavy breathing of the blacksmith under the big pecan tree where they had spread their blankets.

He wished with all his heart he was back in Virginia with the familiar sounds of early morning Richmond coming through his window. But here was only the hard ground under his head and there was no welcome smell of ham and hot biscuits.

He tore his mind from the past. Somehow he must get money to take his mother back home. Surely, he thought, by selling the wagon, horses and household goods, there would be enough. And the lot. That was it. They could sell the town lot.

But first, he'd slip away while Mr. Wilson still slept and look over his property. Well, not exactly his, but at least part of it was. And Mom would be surprised and pleased that he was doing something instead of looking down in the mouth.

Quietly he put on a clean blue shirt and wiggled his long feet into the black leather boots that had been so new and shiny when he left Virgina. Charcoal looked at him eagerly from the end of the stake rope, but Page shook his head and walked softly through the wet grass to the road.

Block three, lot nine. That would be to the right about halfway down to the wagon yard. As he left the smithy his step quickened and he felt better in spite of himself.

A potlikker hound ran out and sniffed at his feet, his growl subsiding as Page rubbed his scarred ears. No one was up yet. The chimneys had only a faint curl of smoke from banked fires.

As he looked at the cabins he decided the owners must be very poor indeed. Nowhere did he see glass windows. Over openings cut in the rough logs hung buckskin, cloth, or crudely split logs on leather hinges. Only one house was more than a single room and a lean-to. This one was a double dwelling with a breezeway or dog trot connecting the two cabins.

Page walked on, counting carefully as he went, "seven, eight—" There it was, a large area on the east side of the road, heavily shaded with live oaks and pecans, dotted with patches of bluebonnets and red flowers that looked like paint brushes.

His spirits rose. Mr. Fairfax had sure picked out a nice place for a home and an academy, except of course there wouldn't be any now. He wondered what a lot like that was worth in silver dollars. He'd have to ask Mr. Wilson.

Feeling a certain pride of ownership, Page left the road and started through the tall grass. Suddenly a rock sang close to his head. He ducked and peered through the murky light ahead of him. Then he saw the strange dwelling rising out of some underbrush. Half tent, half brush arbor, it was surrounded by litter and castoff gear. An old wagon with a broken wheel stood to one side. Tied carelessly to a tree were a skinny mule and a spavined horse.

As the morning light brightened, Page could make out the whole sorry picture—squatters. He knew now why Marker Wilson had insisted they stay the night with him and find the lot later. He stood uncertainly, wondering what his father would have done.

Before he could decide, a burly boy about his own age, with a shock of unruly red hair, sprang from behind the lopsided wagon and swaggered toward him, a rock in one hand, a heavy stick in the other.

"Get out and stay out or I'll clout you one! Thought

you'd sneak in and steal my horse, didn't you?" he sneered, his blue eyes blazing.

Page stood his ground. "I had no thought of stealing your horse. I have one of my own. This lot happens to belong to me. I came down to look at it."

The boy grinned slyly and called over his shoulder. "Hey, Pa, here's a little runt says he own this lot!" He took in Page's leather boots, butternut pants, and clean blue shirt and wiped his mouth with a dirty sleeve. "Real fancy Dan, ain't you?"

Before Page could answer, a bald headed, grizzly little man crawled out of the rubble of brush and blankets, blinking his red-rimmed eyes and hitching up ragged pants. "Git out before I whale you one. Strangers ain't welcome here. I'll have ya run outa town!"

As the scrawny little man lurched toward him, ranting and clutching at his tobacco stained beard, Page realized he would have to run or fight, two against one. And the boy outweighed him by twenty pounds.

He knew his father would have tried to reason with the squatters, but there was no time left. Fear tightened his stomach as the distance closed. He had never been much good at rough-and-tumble fighting. There had never been need for it.

He could see the freckles on the boy's face now and sense the power behind those flexed muscles. As he saw the club raised, he ducked and kicked with his sharp-toed boot at the boy's grubby shins.

Caught off balance and yelling with pain, his attacker stumbled backward against a tree stump and went sprawling. Page darted toward him, fists raised. Then he saw a bald head coming at him like a battering ram. The breath went out of him as he hit the ground. He could smell tobacco, rum, and sweat as the man fell on top of him and reached for his throat.

Vaguely Page heard hoofbeats, then wild shouting. He caught a glimpse of a powerful arm that snatched the bearded little man and swung him like a plucked chicken in mid-air.

The horse was pulled up so sharply dirt flew into Page's face. He couldn't see the man in the saddle but he recognized Marker Wilson's voice. "You, Pat Regan. You'll answer for this!"

Page stumbled to his feet in time to see the boy streaking into the woods. "Thanks, Mr. Wilson. I didn't know these folks were here. They seem to think the lot is theirs."

Marker Wilson dropped the elder Regan to the ground like an empty meal sack. The man tried to back away but the smith turned his bay in front of him.

"Don't move or I'll ride you down. This boy is Page Carter. His pa was to be the new schoolmaster here, but he died afore he got here. Mrs. Carter and Page have got the rightful deed to this lot. You thought when Benton Fairfax got killed you could move in here and take over.

You didn't know Fairfax had sold this lot to the Carters, did you?"

"He was fixin' to steal my horse," the old man whined.

"None of your lies, Regan. Not even a thievin' Comanche would steal that sorry nag of yours."

"Red said he was horse thievin'," Regan insisted.

The blacksmith climbed out of his saddle and grabbed the little man by his ragged beard. "Don't blame it on your son. You and Red pack up your gear and be out of here by noon. The Carters are putting their wagon here tonight."

"My wagon's broke, Marker. I ain't got nowhere to go."

"Then fix it. Be the first day's work you've done in a year. And I'll give you somewhere to go. You and Red pitch your wigwam on my farm a mile down the road. I'll stake you to some grub if you'll chop some cotton."

"I ain't a-workin' for no one," Regan protested.

Marker gave his beard another twist. "Get out, before I tell the town you jumped this boy, two against one!" He gave the man a shove toward the wagon and forked his saddle.

"Light up behind me there, Page. Your ma'll have breakfast ready and getting cold. Sorry you run into those trashy folks. I meant to get them off first thing come sunup, but you got here first."

Page tried to forget how sore his middle was. "I guess that boy won't forget he didn't finish his fight with me."

"No, I reckon not. Those Regans never forget any-thing. Always a chip on their shoulder. The old man is a sorry critter, not worth shooting. Spends what he can get in the 'doggery' on rum. That boy, Red, might turn out pretty good if he'd ever listen to anyone except his pa."

"Doesn't he learn anything at school?"

"Land almighty, son! He never had any learning in his life. I expect the Regans are about the only family in town don't own a Bible."

As Page slipped down from the bay in front of the blacksmith shop, Marker Wilson tied his horse to a post oak. "I'm afraid a lot of young'uns will grow up to be just like Red Regan if we don't get us a school here, and a church."

"There's no church either?"

"Seems like everyone is so busy trying to get a roof over his head and clearing land and planting cotton and fighting Indians, we haven't got us one built yet. We have Sunday meeting at Judge Anderson's—the double cabin down the road—but it don't seem quite the same as a real church with a steeple and a bell."

Page suddenly realized his own troubles were not quite so big. All the people in Serena had problems aplenty, he guessed.

Susan Carter's voice came from the back cabin, "Break-fast is ready!"

The smith caught Page by the arm. "Let's don't tell

your ma about the Regans. She's a brave lady, but she's had her share of grief."

Page nodded and brushed the dirt off his shirt. He must remember to ask Mr. Wilson how much boat fare would be to Virginia.

As they sat down on the rough benches around the homemade table that was sanded to satin smoothness, Mrs. Carter placed a tin plate of beans and corn pone before each of them.

"Would you ask the blessing, Mr. Wilson?"

Marker Wilson moved uneasily on the split log bench, and his ruddy face took on a deeper color. "No one ever asked me to say the blessing, ma'am—"

Susan Carter smiled encouragingly, folded her hands, and bowed her head. Page was mortally certain his beans were going to be stone cold, but finally came the hesitant voice from the big kindly man who had taken in two strangers.

"Lord, will you please bless these beans and the fine lady who cooked them, and the boy here, who got up a mite too early this morning for his own good. Amen."

Page Carter felt some of the worry go out of him. He knew he had found a stalwart friend in Marker Wilson.

CHAPTER THREE

Stars For A Roof

When the blacksmith had gone to his shop in answer to the impatient call of a farmer, Page staked out the horses to graze in a nearby meadow and gave Charcoal a bit of corn pone from his pocket. He tidied up the wagon and went back to the cabin where his mother was setting the place to rights.

"It beats me," Susan Carter said, "how a lone man like Mr. Wilson can keep such a neat place." She put the clean tin plates and finely carved wooden spoons on the shelf above the wash bench.

Page never noticed such things unless a place was dirty. As he looked around the snug cabin, his respect for Marker Wilson grew. The puncheon floor was fitted and calked to perfection. No daylight could be seen through careless chinking of the log walls. In one corner stood a fine old chest of drawers. In the other was the wide bed braced solidly against the two walls and supported on the third side by a log leg.

"You've no idea how comfortable this bed was, Page," his mother said as she tucked the rough homespun sheets around the mattress above the sturdy rope springs.

Page stared at the wide fireplace with the two long rifles and powder horn hung on wooden pegs above it. He must have Mr. Wilson show him how best to load a gun quickly. He had used his father's rifle a few times, but he didn't like killing things. Living in Richmond where game could be bought at the market, the Carters had had little use for a long rifle.

"Mr. Wilson seems to be mighty handy," Page admitted. "Mom, I think we had better make our plans to go back to Virginia—that is, if you want to."

Susan Carter sat down in the hide-bottomed chair by the fireplace. "Yes," she agreed, seeing the boy's anxious face. "There is nothing here for us. One day Texas will be a good place to live in, but we must support ourselves now, Page, and I doubt either of us could turn an honest dollar in Serena."

Page felt relieved. At least his mother didn't want to stay, either. "First thing," he planned aloud, "is to find a buyer for our town lot. Then I'll find someone who will pay a good price for the horses and wagon." His face clouded as he thought of selling Charcoal, the mare he had ridden since he was ten.

"We'll sell the household goods, too," Susan added. "People have so few things here that the bed and chest and desk should bring a good price."

Page could see from his mother's face that parting with the fourposter and father's desk came just as hard for her as selling Charcoal did for him. "I'll buy you things when we get back to Richmond, Mom." He tried to sound convincing, but he wondered what kind of job he could get at his age.

Susan took off her calico apron and folded it carefully. "Mr. Wilson said we had better call on Judge Anderson and see that our lot deed is in order. He lives in the double cabin a block down."

As he helped his mother over the deep wagon ruts of the road, Page was aware that the village had come to life for the day. Children shouted and romped. Wash pot fires spiraled from back yards where women were boiling clothes. Men with rifles passed them, headed for the woods and a bag of game. A few farm wagons lumbered toward the store.

Everyone "howdied" in friendly fashion and not a few admiring glances were cast at Susan Carter as she stepped daintily through the dust in her proper black bonnet and second best dress.

"I guess word got around we've come to town, Mom," Page said as they turned off the road.

"In a town of two hundred where strangers seldom stop, I expect everyone knows all about us down to the last quilt in the wagon!" Susan smiled at the puzzled look on Page's face. "At least they don't throw rocks at us. They're friendly people."

Page wondered what his mother would say if she had seen the ruckus before breakfast.

"Now mind your manners, Page," she told him.

The request made Page feel as though he were back in the parlor in Richmond, with the headmaster coming to tea. Even on the frontier, Mom didn't change.

He grinned as they neared the cabin. "Look, Mom, flowers in the yard, just like you had at home."

"Why, there are!" Susan exclaimed. "These folks must be living here quite a while."

Before they could knock, a straight-backed, white-haired man opened the massive door. "Good morning, madam. You are Mrs. Carter and you are the son, I presume. Mr. Wilson told me all about you. Come in, and welcome to Serena."

With the courtly manners Page had seen so often among the lawyers of Virginia, Judge Anderson ushered them into his office which occupied one side of the double cabin. "I was away when you drove in last night," he went on, "or I should have had my wife offer our hospitality for the night."

Page shook hands with the judge and seated his mother in front of the fine mahogany desk. "Thank you, sir. We fared very well with the smith. Mr. Wilson and I slept under the pecan tree back of his shop. I'm so used to sleeping in the open, I'm afraid a bed would feel passing strange to me!"

Judge Anderson stroked his white goatee with a fragile hand. "Well, when you get your cabin built, you'll get used to a bed again, young man."

"We aren't staying, Judge," Susan Carter announced. "With my husband's death, and the passing of Benton Fairfax, our plans have had to be changed."

"My deepest sympathy, ma'am," the judge said quietly. "I can understand your wish to return to Virginia. If I can help you with your plans—let's see, the stage coach to Galveston runs once a week, in dry weather that is. Then a ship to New Orleans and passage from there to the east coast."

It was a comforting thought to Page—passage home, but he also knew it sounded very expensive. "First, sir," he said, "we will have to sell our horse, wagon and gear and our town lot to pay for our fare to Richmond. How much does the whole passage cost?" His tone was uneasy. He wasn't used to discussing large sums of money.

The judge's brow furrowed in thought. He looked at the slender dark-haired woman and the gangling boy who had already outgrown his homespun pants. "For the two of you," he said slowly, "the passage would be around two hundred dollars."

To Page this seemed a staggering lot of money. "Well, we aim to sell all we have and——"

"You have no ready cash, ma'am?"

"No, Judge," Susan Carter said. "We have only twenty dollars in gold. But surely the horses and wagon would bring——"

The judge shook his head. "The truth is, ma'am, that is more hard money than most of us in this town have to our names."

"But, Judge," Page protested, fear running over him like cold water. "Surely there is——"

"No, there isn't, son. There isn't anyone in this town I know of who could buy your horses, wagon, or lot even if they had need for them. This has been a hard year for cotton and corn. The Indian raids wiped out a lot of families and took a lot of stock. Everyone is poor."

Susan clasped her hands tightly in the folds of her sprigged cambric skirt. "But how can anyone live without *some* money?"

The judge leaned back in his chair and smiled ironically. "I used to think it impossible, too. I came from Kentucky five years ago. I learned very quickly about the barter system. For instance, I traded some town lots for having this cabin built. My fees are paid in produce—game, fish, bacon, honey—whatever my client has that I have need of."

Page let his mouth drop open in wonder. "And you never really see any money, sir?"

The judge nodded. "That's about it, son. Usually cotton from my farm brings in enough hard cash to buy coffee, sugar, and shoes for the family, but the Indians burned my cotton this year and—well, you can see for yourself." He stuck out his feet in home-made moccasins. "I admit they don't go very well with my beaver hat, but on the frontier most of us are in the same boat!"

Susan tried to smile, but Page could see that it came hard. No passage home! At least until he could earn some real money somewhere to pay their fares.

He scarcely saw his mother showing the deed to the town lot. He heard only vaguely the assurance of the judge. "Yes, the deed is in order. Well, I should say the lot, if anyone had money to buy it, would be worth around twenty-five or thirty dollars at the most. Now I want you to meet my family, ma'am, and do us the honor of having dinner at our table."

Page felt trapped. He couldn't just sit and let the bitterness roll over him. He was suddenly homesick and afraid and lonely. He couldn't face strangers at a dinner table and make his manners and pretend he wanted to stay in Texas.

But you didn't just bolt and run, not from the home of a gentleman who had shown every kindness. The courtesy drilled into him from early childhood made him rise and shake hands with the judge. "Thank you, sir, for your advice. My mother would like to stay for dinner, I am sure, but I must see Mr. Wilson and get the wagon and gear moved to our lot. Will you excuse me, please?"

Holding himself tightly in check, he walked from the cabin and measured his steps numbly down the road, seeing nothing, responding stiffly to the greetings of those who passed.

When he had almost reached the blacksmith shop, the trapped feeling was too much. He broke into a run. Snatching the flute from the open trunk in the wagon, he threw his saddle on Charcoal, who pranced happily to be ridden again. With his head down and the taste of salty tears in his mouth, he spurred his horse up the road to the north. Where? He didn't know and didn't care.

Charcoal ran easily for half a mile before Page realized the road had become a deserted wagon trail through heavy woods. He pulled up the mare and turned off beneath spreading pecans and oaks draped with swaying grey moss. Smaller dogwood trees showered their white blossoms in his face as he brushed against them, and the deep pink redbud branches gave way as he rode slowly into a clearing.

Heavily he slipped from the saddle and tied Charcoal to a sapling. He dropped down on a fallen log, velvety with green moss, and let a sob startle the squirrel in a nearby tree.

He looked at the flute in his hand as though surprised to find it. His father's flute. He knew now why he had brought it with him. Always when his father was tired or worried, Jefferson Carter had taken his flute to the little garden in back of the brick house. There he had played until trouble was banished by the music.

Never had Page touched the flute until they started to Texas. Then, when the daylight hours were tiresome or the rainy nights long, Jefferson Carter had taught his son to play. Page had found it fun to place his lips against the cool silver and draw notes from the pipe by moving his fingers over the holes. But he had learned only one tune, "Come to the Bower."

Now he lifted the flute and started to play. The music seemed to draw the tightness from his face. His heart eased with the liquid notes. He didn't even hear the crackle of twigs when Marker Wilson pulled up his horse and peered through the oak leaves. But he knew someone was there and put down the flute.

"It's only me, Page," Marker said. "Saw you light out on Charcoal. Just remembered I hadn't warned you not to go out of town alone without a rifle. Not many Indians since the raid, but a few Comanches hang around, hoping to steal a good horse. Wouldn't go any further than this alone or unarmed."

"Thanks, Mr. Wilson. I was so upset, I never thought of that."

"Mighty sweet sound you make on your—what is it? Can't recollect I ever heard one."

"That's my father's flute. He taught me to play a little. And it's like he said. 'Don't bother the world with your troubles. Let them come out of a flute and blow away.'"

"Your pa was right, son." Marker sat down on the log and began splitting a twig. "Same with all of us, I guess.

Now me, when I get good and riled up or sorrowed over something, I take it out swinging that hammer until the clang of the anvil wakes the dead. What so mortally upset you?"

Page found he could talk about it calmly now. "Judge Anderson explained how no one has any hard money. So I can't sell any of the gear. We won't have money for passage home. I guess we have to stay in Texas until I can earn some. But two hundred dollars is—well, I just don't think I can ever get that much. I don't know what to do."

Marker chewed on the twig in silence. "Figured that's what you'd run up against. Just got to face it. You're between the rock and the hard place. But we've all been there, boy."

"It's Mom I worry about most. How will she manage?"

Marker drew a deep breath. "Page, it's up to you to manage, not your ma. Back east you weren't grown up. But out here on the frontier—well, it sure separates the men from the boys."

"Yes, sir. But it seems a little new for me to be taking care of Mom."

"I know, she always took care of you. Now you got to figure something out that will work. What can you do best?"

Page drew marks in the grass with his boots. "You might as well know, Mr. Wilson. I'm a poor shot with a gun. I don't like to kill. I'm no good with my hands, building things and such. About all I can do is read, and spell and figure. I graduated from the academy last year two years ahead of my class. I helped some with the beginners."

Marker slapped his smoke-stained britches. "The Lord couldn't of sent you to a better place, son. We need a schoolmaster worse than plowshares in Serena. Everyone was so disappointed when they heard about your pa, for they'd been planning on their young'uns to get some learning."

A look of amazement came over Page's face. "I couldn't run a school, Mr. Wilson. I'm only fifteen. I'm no schoolmaster!"

It was plain to see Marker Wilson had made up his mind. "You saw all those shirttail boys running and hollering this morning. Wild as Indians they are. Some of them twelve years old and never had a day in school. We don't want them growing up like that, never reading or writing or figuring. You could teach them, Page. I know almighty well you could."

"But there's no school house," Page protested. "I don't even have a roof over my head. They'd laugh me down."

"Anyone who laughs at a schoolmaster in Serena can answer to me," Marker said angrily. "Now, I know this barter system instead of money sounds strange to you, but it works out. You want to sell your two farm horses. Suppose I take the horses and build you a cabin in return.

I mean a double cabin where you could keep school on one side and live in the other."

"But you can't sell the horses either."

"No, but I can trade them for scrap iron I need real bad to build Colonel Knight a cotton gin down the river."

"How could pupils pay their tuition?"

"Just like they pay everyone else—in whatever they have. You could get pigs, turkeys, venison, a little farm land, mebbe a cow. When times get better you might even get paid some in silver dollars."

The sound of silver dollars had its effect on Page. "Why, I'll bet in a few years I might save enough to get us back to Virginia. Let's talk to Mom about it!"

At the supper table, Page and Marker poured out their plans to Susan Carter, who listened gravely, obviously proud of her son. "I think your plan is wise, Page. You aren't too young to teach. I remember your father talking about a William McGuffey he met when he visited the University of Virginia last year, the man who was writing a speller and reader. Mr. McGuffey moved to the frontier of Ohio when he was younger than you are. There was such need of schoolmasters that he taught school at the age of thirteen."

The trade of horses for building a double cabin was arranged and Susan Carter and Page made ready to move onto their property and live in the wagon until it was ready. While his mother closed the trunk, Page whispered to Marker Wilson, "Did those squatters move off?"

"Yes, I saw to it they were gone by noon. Don't worry your ma with it."

"No sir." Page climbed on the wagon. "Thank you for your kindness. We'll do fine now."

As they drove onto the lot and halted the wagon under the moon-drenched trees, Page no longer felt angry and bitter. "You sleep in the wagon, Mom. I'll put my quilt under the tree."

CHAPTER FOUR

Page Makes A Bargain

The next few days seemed to Page the busiest he had ever known.

He moved the wagon to the back of the Carter lot to insure as much privacy as possible from the road. Here there was underbrush and tangled vines to be chopped down and cleared away. As the axe blistered his hands and sweat rolled down his bare back, he came on some tattered pieces of tarpaulin and old blanket. He wondered what had become of the redheaded boy and his father who had only a week ago called this lot their home. But he forgot about them when his mother called from the wagon, which she had turned into a crowded but neat little bedroom. "Page, could you go to the store?"

Page put on his shirt and wiped his face on an old tow sack. "Shall I pay cash or charge it?"

Susan looked thoughtfully at the five dollar gold piece

in her hand. "I doubt if they will give us credit, Page, but try anyway. Here's the list, just what we can't do without —coffee, sugar, salt, beans, bacon. The meal will hold out for a few days."

A few wagons were tied in front of the store with its sign "J. Williams, Prop." Several old men sat on the wide steps, whittling. From the open door came the familiar mingled smell of tobacco, spices, bacon, and leather.

As Page stepped inside, he could see in the dim light of several small windows the long plank counter supported by two hogsheads. Behind it were shelves sparsely stocked with coffee, tea, ginger, raisins, and chocolate.

He could make out the barrels of sugar and salt, sacks of beans and slabs of bacon with a few cured hams dangling from ceiling hooks. Other shelves across the room held a jumbled assortment of cotton yard goods, axes, hatchets, knives, saws, shovels and candlesticks.

The round, fat storekeeper left off haggling over some hides and came to ask Page his pleasure. All eyes in the store turned on the new customer.

Having read off his list, Page waited while Mr. Williams banged the staples down on the counter with the assurance that his goods were the best to be had on the Brazos. "Where's your tow sack?" he asked.

Page realized he had made a mistake. Of course he should have brought a sack. This wasn't Richmond where groceries were delivered to the back door. "Sorry sir, I forgot to bring one," he said lamely.

"Well, never mind, here's an extra one." Mr. Williams stuffed the staples into the sack and waited.

Page saw the sign over the counter "Prompt pay only. Cotton and Hides accepted." At least he could try. "I am Page Carter, sir," he told the storekeeper. "My mother and I are having a cabin built on our lot down the road. I would like to open an account with your firm."

He had been with his father once when he opened an account at a new store. Page was sure he had said the right thing. But he could hear laughter from the steps.

Mr. Williams rubbed his pink hand over his equally pink balt spot. "Glad to know you, Mr. Carter. Happy to have you trade with us. You folks dealing in cotton or hides?"

Page could feel the color coming up in his face. "No, sir. We're just getting a start here."

Mr. Williams did not laugh or even smile. "Sorry, boy, it will have to be cash." The loafers who had gathered round the counter were silenced by the frown thrown in their direction, but their eyes bulged as Page slowly took the gold piece from his pocket and laid it on the counter.

The storekeeper himself seemed startled. "First gold I've seen in a year, Mr. Carter." He hurried to the back of the store. When he came back, he handed Page three silver dollars and some change.

When Susan Carter heard there would be no credit at the store she made the best of it. "Never mind, Page. This will last us for a long time. It's just meat I worry about. Do you suppose you could shoot a rabbit or squirrel in the woods? That seems to be the way other people get their meat."

Page went back to clearing the lot and tried not to think about hunting. He rigged up an outdoor oven of sorts with stones and fixed forked stakes with a rod over it for the iron kettle. As he worked, he heard snatches of conversation from the shade of the wagon where Susan Carter entertained Judge Anderson's wife and Mr. Williams' sister with all the graciousness of a Richmond lady in her parlor.

"It won't take Marker Wilson long to build a cabin," Miss Williams was saying. "But meantime, why don't you have your boy fix you a brush arbor where you can eat if a shower comes up? We still use ours in summer."

"Brush arbor?" Page thought. "Whatever is that?" Quietly he laid down his axe and hurried off the back way to the Williams' house. Skirting the rear of the property he saw now what she meant. A summerhouse, but not white latticed and covered with grapevines like the one his grandmother had in Virginia. This was made of four stout saplings with narrow poles laid across the top. Over the poles was piled dry brush as a sort of thatch. Benches inside made an open summer room.

He circled back home. Surely he could build a simple thing like that without asking Marker Wilson's help. While the ladies drank their tea from Susan's best china cups, Page went to work with a will.

But it wasn't as easy as it had looked. He used his own height as a yardstick and notched the saplings with his knife a foot above his head. From the back of the lot he cut four larger saplings and four smaller ones. Without searching too far, he came back with eight narrow poles about two inches in diameter. Stepping off a six by six area, he dug holes at the four corners and set the big saplings upright.

In his haste he hadn't dug the holes very deep, for the ground was hard. The posts seemed to wobble a bit, so he piled rocks around them until they seemed solid.

Using a barrel for a ladder, he hoisted up the smaller crosspieces and suddenly realized he had no nails. For a moment he was stumped. Then he took his saddle from a tree fork and stripped off some of the long leather fringe. He felt pretty proud of himself as he tied the crosspieces to the tops of the posts with the leather thongs.

Carefully then, he laid the narrow poles across the framework and tossed the brush he had cleared over them. It was almost sundown as he climbed wearily to the ground and stepped back to look at the first thing he had ever built alone.

His heart sank. It was all wrong. One side was lower than the other and it looked like it might fall down at any minute. He stood there, defeated by his own lack of skill. He didn't hear Susan Carter's soft footsteps.

"Why, Page, a brush arbor just like Miss Williams was

talking about! You did it all alone. However did you figure out how it was made?"

He shook his head. "It's crooked and it's shaky. But I wanted you to have one, Mom."

"Page, to me it looks wonderful. Come on, let's move our table in here and eat."

"You really like it, Mom?"

Page wasn't tired now. He didn't care if his hands hurt and his back was sunburned. He had really built something.

As they finished their supper, Marker Wilson rode in to pay his respects.

"Come on into the arbor for coffee, Mr. Wilson," Susan called. As Marker entered, he brushed his heavy shoulder against one of the four posts. The brush slid, the roof poles fell, and the whole arbor collapsed on the three people inside.

Marker poked his head through the debris and stared at Susan, who wore an oak brush crown tilted over one ear. Page came up for air with the coffee pot in one hand and a roof pole caught in one of his boot tops.

For a moment no one spoke. "Are you hurt, ma'am?" Marker asked with concern.

Susan looked at Page and then at the smith. "I'm quite all right—but I've lost the sugar bowl!"

Marker Wilson's laughter roared through the treetops and down the road. Susan tried to get up, but it was just too much. She laughed until the tears ran down her cheeks.

But to Page it wasn't funny. It was crushing defeat at the end of a frustrating, weary day. He struggled free and would have walked away in the twilight if Marker hadn't stopped him.

"Come here, Page. Mebbe I don't know you well enough to say this, but I'll chance it because I think a mighty lot of you and your ma. You worked on this most all day, didn't you? And when it fell down, you were hurt all over. That right, son?"

"I guess so," Page said stiffly.

Marker began to stack the fallen poles against a tree. "You're going to live on the frontier, boy. You'll have to learn to do a lot of things you never did before. It won't be easy. But first you'll have to learn to laugh at your own mistakes and start over. I laughed because we all looked so danged funny. And I laughed because when I came to Texas five years ago, the first thing I ever built didn't turn out so well either."

"It didn't?" Page asked in amazement.

"No," Marker chuckled. "I made a bear trap and ended up getting my own foot in it!"

Page looked at the big blacksmith with a leather thong draped over one ear and dry oak leaves standing upright in his hair. Suddenly the hurt was gone and he too could laugh. "I'll dig the post holes deeper, Mr. Wilson! The next one I build won't fall down in your coffee!"

True to his word, Page spent the next day carefully measuring, hammering, and sawing. When he had finished, he was proud of his brush arbor. He knew it was straight and solid.

He had time left to go fishing with Judge Anderson, who showed him a grassy bank of the Brazos where catfish almost begged to be caught. But after a few days of the same diet, Page knew they could not eat fish forever. He saw other men and boys bringing in turkey, rabbit and even venison.

There was no way to put off hunting any longer. He had made a garden and planted the seeds given to Susan by friends and neighbors. The lot was tidy. The horses were watered and staked out to pasture.

Grimly he took his father's long rifle, shot bag, and powder horn from the wagon and told his mother he was going hunting, just as though he were used to bringing in meat every day of the year. He didn't know where to go and was too proud to ask. He took the faint trail off the road where he had seen other hunters disappear.

A rabbit scuttled across the path. He heard squirrels set up a chatter in the trees above him. A deer bounded from a thicket as he passed. He tried to walk quietly, but his boots made every twig crackle.

In the first small clearing, he sat down on a stump and tried to remember what his father had said about loading the old rifle. Carefully he measured out the powder and poured it into the long barrel. Then came the patch around the bullet. He tamped it down on the powder with the long ramrod.

Quietly he stood up and looked into the big pecan tree where he had heard the squirrels. He saw a flash of grey fur, then another. Raising the heavy rifle to his shoulder he sighted cautiously along the barrel. There was the squirrel, looking down at him with bright, inquisitive eyes. He swallowed hard and pulled the trigger.

The gun kicked violently against his shoulder, nearly knocking him to the ground. The shot went wild. The squirrels scurried away.

Page rubbed his shoulder and patiently reloaded his gun. Five times he shot, but the bullets hit only the tree trunks or shattered the tender green leaves. His shoulder ached and his arms were tired. One more shot and he'd have to go home empty handed. He moved farther into the woods and saw a wild turkey raise its head from behind a fallen tree.

His hopes soared. He could just see himself walking down the road in town with the turkey carelessly over his shoulder. He could almost hear his mother's delighted surprise!

With dogged determination he aimed, holding himself stiff against the recoil of the rifle. The shot rang out in the still woods. The turkey whirred upward. Suddenly, another rifle barked. The turkey dropped to the ground.

Page was stunned. His first thought was Indians. He

stood frozen in the deep grass, not knowing whether to run or try to reload his rifle.

A shock of red hair showed across the clearing. "Ya," a voice taunted. "You couldn't hit the side of a barn!"

Page felt shame and humiliation pour over him. He watched Red Regan pick up the fat turkey and swagger off through the woods. He knew his clumsy efforts had been watched. He knew the whole town would hear about it before he got home. And he had nothing for supper.

He wondered how they were going to live until he could get his school started and trade his teaching for meat on the table. He guessed he'd have to swallow his pride and tell Mr. Wilson what a poor hunter he was. Perhaps he could learn from the blacksmith how to bring down game with one shot.

When he reached the smithy, he found Marker Wilson was not alone. A well-dressed gentleman with a tall beaver hat and a ruffled shirt stood impatiently in the doorway, waiting for his horse to be shod.

Page melted into the shadows back of the forge as the big hammer beat out the white-hot metal. Finally the work was finished and the gentleman in fine clothes turned to Marker. "How much do I owe you? My bill has run several months, but I want to settle up before I go to San Antone."

Marker's face was dark with effort. "That's four horses shod, new bit, that plow straightened——" he seemed to give up. "I guess you owe me four dollars, Colonel Gregg."

The Colonel smiled. "Have it your way, Marker." He tossed four silver dollars on the bench and cantered off down the road.

Page did some quick addition in his head. He knew it cost a dollar to shoe a horse, plus the bit and plow. Marker Wilson had been cheated!

"Mr. Wilson, why did you let that man beat you out of two dollars?"

The smith wiped sooty hands on his leather apron. "Don't know as I did," he said. "Colonel Gregg always lets me name the figure."

"But you didn't add it up right. It would come to over six dollars at least." Page saw the set look on Marker's face. "I'm sorry, sir. I didn't mean to find fault. I just thought you shouldn't be cheated."

Marker glanced around the empty shop, his eyes miserable. "I get cheated a lot, Page." He stared down at his big hands, refusing to meet the boy's eyes. "You see, I never had any schooling. I can't read or figure. That's how come they call me 'Marker.' I can't write out my own name. I have to make a mark."

Page didn't trust his own voice to answer this.

"I knew you'd find out," Marker went on dully. "But you being so educated and your ma such a fine lady, I didn't want to shame you both. I'm sorry, son."

Page found his voice. "I'll teach you to read and write, Mr. Wilson.".

"No, Page. I'm too old to go to school now."

"I don't mean that. I could teach you after work at night. We'd keep it a secret and surprise everyone!"

Marker's face brightened. "You think I could learn by fall so I could sign for my cotton shipment?"

"Sure you could. You're smart enough to learn lots faster than most."

"You'd have to let me pay you for teaching, Page." Marker's voice was eager. "I could keep you in game."

It was an easy way out, but Page knew he couldn't take it. "Funny thing, Mr. Wilson, I came here to ask you to teach me something. Mebbe we could trade it out."

"I already told you how to build that brush arbor. That don't count!"

"You say you're ashamed you can't read or write. You have no right to be. You didn't have a chance at schooling. I'm ashamed I can't shoot straight and bring in my own game. But you see, sir, I never did any hunting before. I just don't know how."

Marker's mouth dropped open in surprise. "You mean you can't shoot ary a thing?"

Page grinned. "No more than you can write ary a word! I teach you to write. You teach me to hunt."

"That's a bargain, son. And you call me 'Marker' same as the others. Since I'm going to learn to write real good, that name 'Marker' don't cut into me like it used to."

CHAPTER FIVE

The Missing Gold

May had crowded April off the river banks and put on a dazzling show of purple water hyacinth, scarlet wild roses, and feathery pink mimosa blooms. The wind in the willows was tangy with salt from the Gulf.

Page was homesick and restless. In Virginia he would be swimming in the old cove, poling downstream in a scow, or racing Charcoal in the big meadow near Richmond. But here in Texas there was no time for idle hours. Even on Saturday, he pulled the bellows for Marker Wilson in exchange for the venison steaks and wild turkey the smith provided.

For Page had not yet learned to kill his own game. Everyone in town knew it. Red Regan had seen to that. Often Page passed a knot of boys only to hear the chant, "Can't shoot and can't fight. Can't do nothing but read and write!"

When Page went hunting with Marker one afternoon the smith held out a new pair of moccasins and said, "Put these on and you won't raise such a noise in the woods. Save your boots for Sunday."

In the clearing Marker made him load and reload, over and over, until Page could measure his powder, put the cloth on his bullet, and ram it into the barrel without half looking.

"I know how to do it, Marker," he protested.

"I know you do, but you have to be faster than that."

"I have plenty of time to hunt."

"I'm not thinking of just hunting, boy. Might come a time when you needed to reload fast, and in the dark. Now, do it again."

"You mean there might be more Indians, Marker?"

"Well, I don't want you scaring your ma none. But there's always a few Comanches around. They won't raid the town unless they really get the wind up and come in a big bunch. Just a pair of Indians is usually out to steal a good horse. Man can bed down with the stake rope of his horse tied to his wrist and find the animal gone the next morning. An Indian thinks that's a good joke on a white man. Keep Charcoal tied up at night near your wagon. Now, rest your gun over this log and it won't kick your shoulder so hard."

Page tried not to think about Indians on the prowl. He steadied his gun and sighted down the long barrel at the target tree.

"Don't *pull* the trigger, son. Just *squeeze* it real gentle like."

Page tried, but the gun jumped. The shot went wild.

"Land almighty, Page. You grab that trigger like you was killing snakes. Watch me do it. Keep your eye on my finger."

So it went day after day until Page felt he couldn't walk down the road with his gun again and come home empty handed. Finally, he and Marker went into the river bottoms, hoping the change of scene might bring him luck.

"Used to be some wild boar down in here," Marker said, picking his way through the underbrush. "I've seen them tear a dog to pieces. Could kill a man mighty quick. All cleaned out now, I guess. Let's get down here back of this log and see if I can scare up some wild turkeys."

Page rested his rifle barrel on the log and listened to Marker a few yards away, imitating a turkey call to bring in the birds. The swamp was quiet. Suddenly Page heard a grunting sound. He froze to his gun as a wild boar broke from the brush a dozen yards away and charged toward Marker, his ugly tusks glistening in the muted light.

"Get him, Page, quick!" Marker shouted.

Page didn't have time to think. He veered his own gun barrel and sighted between Marker and the boar. A split second, then he fired. The boar came down, wounded.

Before it could charge again, Marker Wilson fired the final shot.

"Thought for a minute there I wasn't ever gonna learn to write my name!" The blacksmith beamed at Page. "You sure saved my life with a good shot, son. Shows what you can do when the chips are down!"

Page tried to recall just what he had seen the last few moments. Finally, the whole thing fell into place. "Marker, you *did* have your gun. It was under the brush aimed right at that boar. You took an awful chance. What if I had missed like I usually do?"

Marker scuffed his foot in the mud, sheepish at being caught. "I tricked you, Page, sure enough. But I'll bet you won't ever be afraid to shoot again."

"Thanks, Marker. Truth is, I just don't like killing things. Soon as I get my school started, I'll let someone else do the hunting. Guess we better take that boar back to town to warn people about this swamp."

"Let's take it back to let some of these town rowdies know you can shoot," Marker said. Page realized that the smith was just as proud as he was.

It seemed to Page that half the town gathered round the Carter wagon that night to celebrate. The wild boar meat was tough and stringy but no one minded as they listened to Marker tell the story of the hunt over and over again.

Susan Carter proudly passed the cornmeal "hush puppies." Mrs. Anderson had simmered the turnip greens and Miss Williams produced a basket of *dulces*, pecan sugar candies that were usually saved for Christmas.

Then there was singing and fiddle playing and finally, to please his mother, Page brought out the silver flute. Marker Wilson listened in awe as the thin, liquid notes floated out.

As the crowd began to leave he looked again and again at the flute. "That's just about the sweetest music I ever did hear. Where did your pa lay holt of such a thing?"

"My grandfather brought it from England when he settled in Virginia."

"I mind I heard something like that with a drum down to Nashville once. Only it was a marching tune and real shrill."

"That was a fife," Page explained. "It is much like a flute but is just used with drums. I have my father's fife, too. He used to play in the fife and drum corps in Richmond when they had parades."

"Can you play a fife, too?"

"I don't know, Marker. I've never tried. It's in the trunk somewhere. But this isn't getting on with your lesson. Too tired to go at it?"

"No. If you can learn to shoot, seems like I could get the hang of those letters. Come on, let's get started."

Over the flickering candle in the blacksmith's cabin, the lessons went on, night after night. Page was patient. He knew that for a man of thirty-five who had never studied, learning came hard. Nor would Marker use any of Page's slender supply of paper and pencils. "You save those for your school. I can learn just as good with a piece of charcoal and a pine board."

"Did you have to work when you were growing up, Marker, that you couldn't go to school?" Page asked as he watched the big calloused fingers gripping the charcoal and painfully shaping the letters of the alphabet.

"Never was no school to go to. My ma and pa and eight young'uns lived on hard scrabbly land back East. Ma had some learning, but she died afore I was old enough to learn my letters. Pa was so busy keeping us fed he just read us the Good Book and had to let us grow up ever which way."

"How did you get to Texas?"

Marker stretched his cramped fingers. "Soon as I was twelve I got out so I wouldn't be another mouth to feed. I learned blacksmithing a few years. Then I heard about land that growed crops head high on the Brazos, and I started traveling. Caught a flat boat down to New Orleans and worked in an iron foundry afore I got passage money to Galveston. There, how does that 'M' look, son?"

"That's good. Now make an 'A'."

Marker took up his charcoal again. "You see, Page, if my pa had been mean and ugly like Red Regan's, I reckon I might have been just as ornery as Red is. That's why I can't think too hard of the boy. He just never has had much of a chance. Saw him tonight looking at all of us being friendly together."

"Why didn't you ask him to have some supper, Marker? I don't want to fight with him."

"He isn't fittin' to be around your ma. Besides, he ducked into the trees when I saw him. He wouldn't have come even did I ask him. The way I figure, Red Regan is ashamed of his no-good pa and takes it out on everyone else. Mebbe I can get him to come to your school."

As the days flew by, Page found the hours were not long enough to get everything done. He worked in Judge Anderson's garden in return for vegetables, since his own garden was late starting. He fished and hunted, not for pleasure, but for food.

He stored their good pieces of furniture in the back of Williams' store so the rain would not harm them. Then he went into the woods with Marker and helped to fell trees for the cabin to be built. He knew he wasn't much good with an axe, but at least he could help load the wagon and haul the logs back to town.

He saw to it that Marker was no longer cheated on an account. On a white pine board, he lettered the smith's prices and hung it inside the shop. When Marker admired the fine printing, Page made a larger sign, "Marker Wilson, Blacksmith," with a forge and hammer sketched on each side.

"I never did see a thing I admire so much in all my born days!" Marker exclaimed as Page nailed the sign over the shop door. Back he went to his anvil, muttering to himself in rhythm with the mighty hammer, "A-B-C-

D," and spelling out his name as though he were trying to hammer the knowledge into the horseshoe he was making.

That night he spelled ten words, counted to one hundred without a mistake, and wrote his name with such a flourish the charcoal broke in three pieces.

Page looked up at the scudding clouds as he walked home and was glad his mother was staying the night with Mrs. Anderson, who was ill. It was going to rain hard.

He snugged down the rawhide flaps he had made for each end of the covered wagon and tied Charcoal under a nearby tree. He decided it was too hot to sleep in the wagon. He moved his pallet to the brush arbor, and pulling his waterproof poncho over him, dropped off to sleep, too tired even to dream, as he heard the heavy rain start to fall.

By morning the countryside was washed to a clean, shining green with a cloudless sky that Page thought must stretch to the rim of the world. Somehow the sky had never looked quite so big and endless in Virginia.

He stretched, washed his face and decided to change his shirt before he went to Judge Anderson's. Whistling to himself, he raised the rawhide curtain from the front end of the wagon and poked his head inside to be sure he didn't get his Sunday shirt by mistake.

He couldn't find the shirt. He couldn't find anything. The wagon had been rifled while he slept. Clothes were thrown out of the trunk. Books were torn. Papers were scattered. Sugar was spilled from an open bag. Page held his breath as he opened the little box under the tray of the trunk where the gold pieces were kept. The gold was gone.

CHAPTER SIX

A Thief Leaves Town

For a moment Page could not believe the gold had been stolen. Always the settlers left their cabin doors unlatched. Piles of hides were left unguarded on the wharf. Even the Williams' store was untended at times. In Serena there was no jail. There had never been looting or theft.

He peered out the back of the wagon. The rain had washed away any footprints. With a heavy heart Page put the wagon to rights. Somehow he must find the gold before his mother discovered the only money they had was gone.

Without pausing to saddle up, he threw himself on Charcoal and rode off to the smithy where he found Marker Wilson finishing his coffee. "It's gone, Marker. The three gold pieces we had left!"

Marker hurriedly pulled on his shirt. "Who knew you had gold pieces?"

"Everyone in town, I guess. There were a lot of people in the store when I gave the first one to Mr. Williams, the week we came."

"You didn't hear anything last night?"

"No, it rained hard. Ma was at Judge Anderson's and I slept in the brush arbor."

"When you were in the store buying grub that day, was Pa Regan or Red there?"

Page hesitated. But Marker was looking at him, his eyes dark with anger. "Was he?"

"Yes," Page admitted. "Red was in the store."

The smith's face was stony. "Come on. I know where he'd go to spend it. Don't tell anyone yet. If the town got wind of it the old man would be strung up to the nearest tree. They don't hold with stealing in Serena."

Marker Wilson rode straight for the doggery, which was open for business even though it was only good sun up. Page had never been in a saloon before, but he followed Marker, who shouldered his way through the door.

To Page the doggery looked much like the general store except there were bottles and mugs on the long shelf back of the counter. Mike Dugan came yawning from his breakfast at Marker's call. "Pa Regan or Red been here this morning?"

"You know I don't give no credit, Marker. Pa ain't got

the money to pay for rum. Say, what you so riled up about?"

"Three five dollar gold pieces have been stolen in Serena. Don't give off with any lies, Dugan!"

Mike Dugan looked at Marker's big fist on the counter. "I swear I never sold him nothing! But I did hear scuffling on the road before daylight and someone tried to get me up. Said he wanted rum afore he went to Galveston."

The smith fixed Dugan with narrowed eyes. "Anyone comes here with a gold piece, call me, or I'll break every bottle in the place. Come on, Page."

As they rode past the wagon yard, Marker looked to be sure no strangers had tied up for the night. "It couldn't be anyone but the Regans, Page! I sure hate to think Red would be so lowdown, but we've got to find out."

"Where to now?" Page asked.

"Where would a man go if he had stolen money and wanted to get out of town?"

As if in answer to Marker's question, the *Yellowstone,* the only steamboat on the Brazos, blew for a landing as she nosed into the wharf a block below the wagon yard.

Marker spurred his bay to a trot and Page dug his heels into Charcoal. They tied up their horses and joined the crowd just as the gangplank went down.

A few passengers got off to walk about. Some hogsheads and boxes were unloaded for Mr. Williams. There was a packet of mail for Judge Anderson to distribute, a keg of rum for Mike Dugan, and some scrap iron for Marker Wilson.

But there was no sign of Pa Regan or his son. The crowd melted away and only the loading of hides remained to be done. The stevedores went to work carrying the heavy bundles up the gangplank, almost concealed by their loads.

Page would have turned away, but Marker suddenly lunged across the rough log wharf. "There he is!" Halfway up the gangplank Marker seized a bundle of hides and threw them to the deck with a mighty heave. Beneath the load were Pa Regan and his son.

The old man tried to twist away, but the blacksmith pinned his skinny arm behind his back. "Where is it?" he demanded.

"I ain't done nothing. I got me a job of work. Going to Galveston, I am."

Even as the old man whined his innocence, Red Regan streaked down the gangplank and disappeared into the woods.

"He got away!" Page shouted.

"Red never took it. His pa did." The smith turned back to the little man who cringed in his grasp. "Where are the gold pieces, Regan?"

Regan saw he was caught. "I never took 'em. Red thieved so we could get to Galveston."

Marker shook him as though he were threshing a

pecan tree. "That boy never stole. Hand over the gold or I'll break your arm!"

Page could see a crowd gathering as the smith's voice roared up the road. The captain came running down the gangplank. "If you want to fight, get off and let those hides aboard!"

Marker nodded to the captain. "Got a passenger here for you, Cap, but he has a few things he wants to leave in Serena." Hoisting Pat Regan onto the deck, he grabbed him by the ankles and held him up in midair, shaking him as though he were a possum.

Page watched in amazement. Out of Regan's ragged pants came two bullets, a knife, and dried jerky. The crowd began to laugh. "Where is it?" Marker boomed, giving him another shake. The old man gasped for breath as three gold pieces rolled out on the deck.

Marker tossed him to one side and picked up the gold. He gave it to Page and turned to the captain. "This man wants to work his way to Galveston. And see that he works!"

The blacksmith hitched up his pants and dropped a copper coin at Regan's feet. "If you ever show your face in Serena again, you'll be almighty sorry."

Page held the gold tightly in his pocket. "Thanks, Marker. I'll leave the money with Judge Anderson after this."

By noon everyone in town knew the story. Many thought Red Regan had been the thief.

Page slept uneasily that night with his gun by his side. He heard nothing, but the next morning he found a wild turkey and a haunch of venison on the wagon seat.

"Red Regan didn't steal, Page," Marker Wilson said. "You mark my words, Red tried to make up with this meat for what his father had done."

Spring turned to summer and the thick July heat spread over the land. The cornfields were sere and brown, and the cotton plants reached toward the merciless sun. Horses and cattle hugged the shade and stood knee-deep in the shallow river.

Page was too busy to know or care how hot it was. He and Marker Wilson were working against time to be ready for the house-raising in August. For the past month they had cut and hauled pine logs from Marker's farm up the river, stacking them on the Carter lot, cutting them into eighteen and twenty-four-foot lengths.

Then there was the matter of where the cabin should stand. Long into the sultry night, Page sketched pictures until Susan Carter had decided exactly where it would be built on their lot. Page had to agree that she had chosen the right spot, with a big pecan tree at the back to shade it from the afternoon sun, and twin oaks to the north to break the cold in winter.

"Now," said Marker as they finished staking out the measure of the house, "if we could just find us a good white oak for the shakes, we'd have all the makings."

"Does it have to be white oak?" Page asked.

"Of course. Weathers better than any wood except cypress. Land almighty, boy, I keep forgetting you never did build a cabin before. Set down here a minute with your picture of the house and let me tell you just how this has got to be done."

Page brought the sketch and Marker mapped out work ahead. "Now, this will really be two cabins, each eighteen by twenty-four, joined together with a dog trot or middle passageway under one roof.

"First, we've got to split some of those logs and sort of belly the round side into the ground with the split side up for the floor. At each corner goes a bois d'arc post sunk into the ground even with the log floor. That bois d'arc is the strongest wood there is. Keeps the cabin from sitting smack dab on the ground and rotting the first log laid down."

Page looked at the picture he had made. To him it seemed a very handsome cabin. "You mean that's what we have to do before the house-raising?"

Marker grinned. "That's not all. And don't count on it looking as fine as the picture you drew. Like as not it won't be that pretty, but it will stand for quite a spell."

"What else is there to be done then?"

"All those logs got to be hewn 'til they have four flat edges."

"Be easier to build with just round logs, wouldn't it?"

"Page, I'm not fixing to leave your ma live in an every-which-way cabin. She's going to have a hewed-log house with no cold coming in the cracks."

And that's the way it was. Marker had said the word. Day after he marked the lines on the logs with a piece of chalk. Then he hewed to the line with his foot adze, a tool shaped like a short handled hoe with a heavy blade.

Page watched him standing on the log, pulling backward with the sharp adze as he split off a good clean face from the wood. It looked easy enough, but Page found, when he tried it, that hewing a log took a lot of patience and skill.

"Here," Marker offered. "You do the notching and let me tend to hewing. To fit these logs together as they go up, we've got to put a square notch on the underside of each log. That way it fits over the log beneath it. Called a rough dovetail notch. Were the logs round, not hewn, it would be a plain old saddle notch."

"Does it have to be on the underside of the log?" Susan asked, as she brought them some cold water from the rain barrel sunk in the ground.

"Sure does, ma'am. That way water runs down the corner of the cabin. If it was notched on the top side of the log, the water would collect, like in a cup, and the wood would rot."

After Marker had gone home, Page looked at the staked-out ground and the slowly growing pile of hewn logs. His muscles were strong now. He no longer was sore and stiff after a day's work. His hands were so calloused they no longer blistered.

Susan fingered a rip in his shirt. "Page, you're getting too big through the shoulders for your clothes. You're so burned by the sun you look almost like an Indian!"

She smiled, remembering the thin, white faced boy who had driven onto the ferry four months ago.

Page wondered if he could really learn how to make a square notch. He did learn, but not in a day. Over and over he tried before he won Marker's approval. That was the week Marker discovered a white oak and brought it in for the shingles. For the life of him, Page did not see how anyone could make shingles from the rough barked log which Marker prized so highly.

He watched impatiently as the blacksmith sawed the white oak into two and a half foot lengths and split them open. Marker sat on a stump and braced one of the split logs between a tree trunk and a crude bench in front of him. With a strange tool shaped like an L, and the bottom of the L sharp as an axe, the smith took up his hammer and started pounding against the top of the L.

To Page's surprise, half inch thick shingles or shakes began to split off and fall to the ground. "What do you call that tool?" he asked as the blacksmith paused to get another split log.

Marker ran his thumb cautiously over the fine cutting edge. "That's a froe. Some folks 'rive shakes' with an axe, but I'd a sight rather use a froe. I saw a man upriver that had one and made this myself. Want to try it?"

To his delight, Page found he could "rive the shakes." With every white oak shingle he cut, he could almost hear the rain pattering on his snug cabin roof.

By August, all the work Marker and Page could do alone was finished—the piles of hewn logs, the stacks of shakes for the roof, the supply of purlins or split logs to which the shakes were to be fastened—everything was ready for the house-raising.

Susan Carter wrote out the invitation and Page went to post it in the general store. "House-raising, August 10, Carter lot. Barbecue, fiddle playing, dancing. Come one, come all. Mrs. Jefferson Carter. Page Carter."

When he came back, Marker Wilson had filled the rain barrel from the spring and was chopping firewood. "How about having your arithmetic lesson right here?" Page suggested. "You tell me how many logs we have cut, how many will go into the whole house, then how many will go in each cabin and each wall."

Marker cast about for a shingle to figure on, but Page stopped him. "No, you do it in your head. You don't need to figure it out with charcoal."

The big smith sat down on a log and marched the numbers slowly around in his mind. He pulled at his ear and chewed a split twig to bits. Finally, his face brightened and he jumped to his feet. "Land almighty, Page, I can do it!" The answers he reeled off were right.

"Have your ma come out here and you ask me all over again."

Like a child at closing school day, Marker showed Susan Carter what he had learned. Her words of praise made the blacksmith beam with pleasure.

"Ma'am," he said, as he shouldered his tools to leave, "would you think hard of me if I asked Red Regan to come to the house-raising? If some decent folks would be kind to him, mebbe he wouldn't be so wild and ornery."

"Of course you may invite him, Marker. Page and I would be happy to have him. Surely you know we don't consider him a thief. Bring him along."

"I've got no quarrel with him," Page said. But he had an uneasy feeling that the invitation spelled trouble.

CHAPTER SEVEN

The House-Raising

As Page rolled out of his quilt before daybreak, on house-raising day, he could smell the barbecued beef which Mr. Williams had been slowly turning on spits in the open trenches all night. He saw Susan flying about in her best starched apron, making sure the water barrel was full, the drinking gourds handy, and the long plank tables spotless.

At seven the wagons started to roll in. The men shouted greetings and inspected the hewn logs. The women carried crocks, jars, and pails to the tables. Ham and turkey, jellies, preserves and honey, watermelons, and wash tubs full of late corn appeared like magic.

Babies were left to sleep in the wagons. Hound dogs chased each other around the barbecue pits. Little girls played with their corn shuck dolls, and small boys were thumped on the head for dipping grubby fingers into the honey.

Marker Wilson mounted a stump and read off the names of thirty-two men, dividing them into two teams, one for each cabin. "Whichever team gets their side built first," he bellowed, "gets to dance first on the new floor tonight! You boys carry water. You girls help with the vittles."

A buzz of excitement swept the crowd as each team divided into four sets of workers, one for each wall. Marker brought his big hammer down on an iron bar as a signal and the race was on.

Red Regan had come with the blacksmith, and now Red and Marker took the ends of a foundation log, both of them calling pleasant insults to the other team. Red for once seemed happy, delighted to display his strength.

Page had asked Marker to put him on a team, but the blacksmith had insisted it was custom that he be the host and see that all went well.

So with Judge Anderson, Page moved about the lot. They welcomed folks from the outlying farms and plantations. Page separated two dogs with one bone, and found the mother of a crying baby. Then he spelled Mr. Williams at the barbecue pit and started the boys with their drinking gourds toward the already thirsty workers.

Anxious to see how the building was going, he started away from the water barrel only to be stopped by Mrs.

Belton, whose double chins waggled with pride as she introduced her brother. "Mr. Josiah Bascom, mayor of San Felipe! This is Page Carter. We're building his little cabin today. They've had *such* a hard time, you know."

Page made his manners to the mayor. He liked Mr. Belton, the wagon yard owner, but Mrs. Belton always rubbed him the wrong way, acting as though she owned the town and the Carters were living on charity.

Mr. Josiah Bascom, he decided, was very much like his sister. His beady little eyes in the round doughlike face darted down the loaded tables. His fancy vest strained across his middle as he fiddled with his gold watch chain. It was quite apparent he had come to eat, not to work.

He talked on and on, starting every sentence with "As mayor—" Page finally escaped, wondering what it was like to feel so important!

The sun rose higher and hotter. The men worked steadily now with little jesting as the heavy logs were swung into place. The teams were even when Susan pounded on a tin plate to announce dinner, and the men doused water over their red faces.

The workers were fed first, then the older men and women, the children, the girls who served the food, and finally the dogs. Men sprawled in the shade for a short siesta, and the race was on again.

It was mid-afternoon before Page went back to the

pile of logs to see how the teams were faring. He found the walls were almost completed.

"Here, Page," Marker called, "take my place for a minute. The other team says there's a log missing. I'll be back before our turn comes."

Page stood by the big log with Red waiting at the other end. But Marker didn't come back. "Come on, Carter," Red said. "It's our turn. Take holt."

Page knew he couldn't carry his end of that heavy log. He had tried a month ago with Marker, but it had been too much. Well, perhaps he was stronger now. Nothing to do but try.

He sucked in his breath and heaved up his end. Halfway to the cabin he realized Red was letting him take more than his share of the weight. He struggled on, feeling his muscles pull and the sweat roll down his face.

They were opposite the rain barrel now. Red's back was only a few feet from its sunken rim. Between Red and the barrel stood Josiah Bascom, the pompous mayor, still talking.

Page was never quite sure what happened next. He only knew his hands could no longer hold the log. He felt it slipping, and pushed forward as he dropped it to keep it from falling on his feet. He saw the other end of the log butt Red Regan in the stomach and topple him backward. As he fell, Josiah Bascom was in the way. Page heard a splash. His honor, the mayor of San Felipe was popped into the rain barrel like a cork in a bottle!

Mrs. Belton started to scream. Josiah Bascom gurgled and bellowed, while dogs barked and men came running. Page stood still, horrified at what had happened.

Marker Wilson put his big hand into the barrel and came up with the dripping mayor.

"I'll have you arrested for this," Bascom sputtered at Red Regan. "Scoundrel!"

Mrs. Belton was outraged. "What can you expect of a boy who steals and—"

Marker Wilson dropped the mayor back into the barrel. "Red Regan never stole anything from anyone, ma'am. I'll thank you to keep a civil tongue in your head."

Mrs. Belton's double chins shook with anger. "You—you—blacksmith!"

Someone fished the mayor out again and tried to dry him off. Susan Carter offered her apologies. Page tried to tell everyone it was his fault, not Red's. But Red Regan had disappeared. In public, he had been called a thief.

Mrs. Belton escorted her dripping brother home. Page stood on the stump and tried to quiet the crowd. "I want you to know that the gold stolen from us and returned was not taken by Red Regan. And it was my fault Red Regan fell against the mayor and knocked him into the rain barrel. I dropped my end of the log."

The silence grew, then a ripple of laughter started among the men. "Page," Mr. Belton called, "if you was gonna knock anyone into a rain barrel you couldn't of picked a bigger bag of wind than Josiah Bascom!"

The laughter snowballed into raucous good humor. Page became the hero of the hour for dousing a man no one liked. But he scarcely heard what went on. He knew Red Regan thought he had dropped the log on purpose.

By nightfall the cabin was finished except for the shakes on the roof, the chinking in the walls and the chimney. The moon came up and smiled down on the house Serena folks had raised for Susan Carter and her son. The fiddles tuned up and dancing started on the new puncheon floor. Page led the Virginia reel with his mother, do-si-doed with his guests to the tune of "Money Musk" and "Leather Breeches," and even loaned his boots to Marker who insisted he couldn't rightly make enough noise in moccasins.

Just before daybreak the wagons began to pull out. The men were pleasantly tired, the women still exchanging gossip and recipes. The children slept.

Last to leave was the blacksmith. "I'm sorry about Red," Page said. "If you find him, tell him I didn't mean to shame him in public like that."

"He's out to my farm most likely. I know it wasn't your fault, Page. I'll tell him, but I reckon he won't listen." Wearily Marker put his foot in the stirrup. "Wish I could have got aholt of him when he was littler and gentled him down."

Page wanted to say it was Red's own fault for letting

him carry most of the weight of that log, but the worry on the big man's face made him hold his tongue.

Now that the house was up, Page couldn't rest until it was finished. Through the hot August days he labored on the roof, fastening the shingles to the purlins with leather thongs, overlapping them so no rain would come in.

Then there was the chinking to put between the logs of the walls. Strangely enough, it was Judge Anderson who was the chinking expert in Serena. He had Page bring in a wagon load of red clay from up river, then supervised the mixing with just the right amount of water and Spanish moss.

Page was a little amazed to see the judge remove his beaver hat and his frock coat, and roll his clean linen shirt sleeves up to the elbow.

"Now," the judge directed. "Take a handful of this mixture, like so, and pack it tightly between the hewn logs. If you are careless, you'll find the rain beating in on your back while you toast your feet before the fire. Before it dries, scrape off the excess mud inside and out." He slapped a handful of clay into the crack and stepped back to admire his skill. "Here, you try it."

Page tried. His first efforts were awkward, but in a few hours he and the judge were chinking at almost the same speed, working against time so that the scorching sun would bake the clay to a hard plaster.

Because news of the school Page was to start had

spread through the town, many a father stopped by to lend a hand with the house. "Sure glad to know my boys will get some schooling. Seems like their ma don't have much time to teach them." Another man calked the floors and dog trot because "I never had much learning. I want my young'uns to have some."

Marker Wilson framed the windows, providing split log shutters and heavy doors made of puncheons almost as thick as the floors. After he had attached the big bar which locked the door from the inside, he made a small hole through the wood to the outside.

"Whatever are you doing putting a hole in the door like that?" Page asked.

"I guess you had real locks on your doors where you come from. Didn't you ever hear of 'come see us, the latchstring's out'?"

"Well, yes, but that hole—"

"Look here, son. See this bar I've pegged to the door. It's loose and free so it can be raised up or down. To lock your door at night, you just raise the bar and let it drop into this open topped slot I've put here against the door frame. Can't no one get in lessen you lift up that bar. Now, I tie this piece of rawhide to the top of the bar. Then I drop it through this hole I've made clean through the door. Anyone wants in from outside can pull that rawhide latchstring and it raises the bar inside."

"I never thought of that!" Page exclaimed admiringly.

Marker grinned. "You live on this frontier long enough and you can make almost anything excepting rain or a good cotton crop."

Marker went outdoors, tried the latchstring and called Susan to see how it worked. "Mostly in Serena, ma'am, the latchstring is left out. Folks see a latchstring out and they take it as a friendly sign to stop and visit. But at night—well, pull in the string and let a body knock if he's a mind to come in."

Susan looked around the snug cabin. "Why, it's all done except the fireplace. What about the bricks?"

Marker laughed. "Ma'am, I reckon there's not a brick this side of the Brazos. Your chimney's going to be built of mud and sticks, but it will draw right and cook good."

The next day Marker built a pole framework tied together in the shape of a firebox, funnel, and chimney. He braced the corners with heavy upright timbers and fastened poles and split sticks horizontally to form a latticework.

Page watched anxiously as he whittled wooden pegs to be used for hooks inside the cabin. Finally his curiosity got the better of him. "Won't all that wood burn down when we start our cooking fire?"

Marker laughed. "After all the work I've put on this cabin, I sure don't aim to burn it down first fire laid! This has to have the mud cats on it."

"Mud cats?"

"Sure. Look here." Marker grabbed a handful of red soil from the half full wagon, sprinkled it with water, added a little Spanish moss, shaped it between his big hands into a roll about nine inches long and three inches thick. "There are your ma's bricks! Slap them on that framework, bake in the sun, and your chimney is done."

It looked simple enough, but the chimney took a lot of mud cats. Page remembered the mud pies the little girls used to make in Richmond. The next day, he and Susan gave a mud cat party. Half the little girls in Serena showed up in their oldest clothes and Page showed them how to make mud pies—the right size—while he put them on the chimney as Marker had directed.

In mid-September, even Marker Wilson admitted there was nothing more he could think of to build. The double cabin with its airy dog trot stood new and clean. The huge flat stones used for the steps were smooth and white. The big fourposter, the desk and chest of drawers all stood in the south cabin.

Above the broad mantel hung the long rifle, shot bag and powder horn. The dutch oven and the crane for the iron kettle were ready. The fragile ladderback chairs, the wooden benches and plank table were all in place. And the latchstring was out.

It seemed only right that Marker Wilson be their first supper guest. Susan Carter had set the table with her best china. Lovingly she took out her silver spoons she had not used for so many months.

Supper was almost ready when Page came bursting in the door and saw the polished silver on the table. "Mom, could you put the silver spoons away?"

"But, Page," she protested, "we've always used them, I—"

"I just came from the smithy. Marker's carved a whole set of wooden spoons for a housewarming gift. He thinks you don't have spoons!"

Quickly Susan and Page hid the silver in the chest drawer, replacing it with the battered tin forks and spoons they had used ever since they left Richmond.

Marker Wilson pulled the latchstring just as they finished and came in, neat and tidy with his blue shirt and butternut pants, carrying a package wrapped in wrinkled brown paper. "I thought you might like these, ma'am, for your new house."

Susan took off the paper and spread out the dozen wooden spoons, carved with loving care into perfect shape with a C on each handle. "Why, Marker!" Susan exclaimed with delight. "They are lovely. I was so tired of these old bent ones we've been using!"

Page saw the smith's face light up with pleasure as Susan displayed her new spoons with pride to every visitor who came in bringing gifts for their new home. There was a comb of honey, there were preserves, herbs, potatoes, squash and pumpkins, and even flower seeds for next spring.

That night Susan Carter slept in her own bed for the first time in six months. Page looked about the cabin, blew out the candle, and rolled into his rawhide wall-bed with its mattress of Spanish moss. It seemed strange not to feel the ground under his head, not to see the stars overhead.

But sleep did not come. He kept thinking of Richmond in far away Virginia. The academy would be open now. There would be concerts by the band in assembly hall. Touring dramatic companies would announce the plays to be put on. Perhaps next year, he told himself, we can go back home.

A week later, the fall rains came and the Brazos rolled in an angry torrent down to the sea. The ferry no longer crossed the river. The *Yellowstone* was tied up at Galveston. Serena seemed cut off from the whole world.

Page was sorting out his small supply of books for the school when he heard Judge Anderson halloo the house. He opened the heavy door and the judge shook his wet poncho on the floor. "Need some help, Page. The stagecoach from up river got almost to Serena and bogged down in the mud. Five passengers, two men and three women, managed to get into town on foot. No place for them to stay. I thought maybe you and your mother could—"

"Why, of course, Judge Anderson. Bring them here,"

Susan offered. "Page and I can sleep in the loft and the women can have this cabin. The men can take the school room across the breezeway if they don't mind bedding down on quilts."

The judge looked relieved. "That's mighty kind of you, ma'am. I have kinfolks visiting in my house and there's just no place to put these folks up."

Page and his mother bustled about, making beds and shaking out unused quilts and blankets. The stranded passengers arrived, well dressed but wet, thankful for any place to eat and sleep.

For two days Susan and Page ran a hotel, offering plain but good food and warm beds. When the sun finally came out and the muddy stagecoach rolled up to the cabin, the passengers were high in their praise of Susan's cooking and her gracious welcome.

As the last gentleman bowed his way out, he put into Page's hand a small leather bag. "I know you considered us guests, Mr. Carter," he said. "You have been most hospitable. But I am not new on the frontier. I know that food is scarce. Please accept this from all of us for your kindness. I hope you will hang out a sign, 'Carter Inn.' More and more people will be traveling this road in the years to come."

Page tried to protest, but the driver cracked his whip, the man climbed aboard, and the stage rattled off toward the coast. Slowly he emptied the bag on the table. There were fifteen silver dollars.

Susan was not too happy about taking the money, but she also realized that they were not in Virginia entertaining friends and kinfolks. She swallowed her pride and told Page he might keep it.

"Mom, just think, we could open an inn like the man said and in no time at all we'd have enough money to pay our passage home!"

"Home, Page?"

"Yes, back to Virginia like we planned." Page's eyes sparkled with hope and excitement.

Susan Carter put the kettle on the crane. "If you turn the schoolroom into a place for travelers to sleep, where would you hold school?"

"But Mom, we'd make money much faster running an inn!"

His mother sat down and looked at him thoughtfully. "What about the fathers who helped you build this cabin? What about the children who will not learn to read and write? They are all counting on you, son."

Page was silent. He put the silver dollars in the chest drawer. "I guess you're right, Mom. But being an innkeeper I could *be* someone in town. As a schoolmaster, well—boys my own age don't ask me to hunt or fish or race with them. Already they think of me as someone different."

"Yes," Susan said. "I have seen and I know you are lonely. But we are not all given the same talents, Page. Some can build with their hands. You can build with your mind. Never belittle the skill God has given you as a teacher."

"I guess a schoolmaster never has much money, Mom."

Susan laughed. "No—not unless the schoolmaster wants to run an inn during the summer months!"

A few weeks later Page was to feel paid for his labors in something that wasn't money. Marker Wilson drove by the cabin, his wagon empty. "Just put the last of my cotton bales on the *Yellowstone*. And I did it, Page—I signed my own name and did my own figuring! The captain like to fell in the river, he was that surprised."

CHAPTER EIGHT

Jim Bowie Comes to Town

In the crude schoolroom with its split log desks and stools, and the bookshelves Page had made, Marker Wilson stood and looked around. There were pegs for coats, there was wood stacked by the fireplace, there was a meager supply of pencils and chalk. "Say, I know a man upriver has some slate in his creek bed. Now my cotton is sold, I aim to go up there and bring back a slab you can break into pieces. Young 'uns can use 'em for slates. When you going to give out the starting day?"

Page took a paper from a dogeared speller. "Next week. I'm going down to the store to post this notice now." He paused uncertainly. "I guess Red Regan won't come to school, will he?"

"I tried to tell him you never dropped that log a-pur-

e at the house-raising, but he acts like he don't be-
ve it. Heard tell his pa is back again but Red keeps
out of town."

Page said what was really on his mind. "What if the
others don't come? What if they don't like me, or think
I'm too young to teach?"

"No cause to be worrying, son. Nary a soul ever tried a
new thing but what some folks wasn't satisfied. You got
to lift up your head and keep traveling, just like your ma
does. Now you get that paper up."

Page took the poster and rode slowly down to the
store, hoping few people would be around so early in the
morning. The usual crowd of boys his own age were
knife throwing at a target near the steps. One of them
was Red Regan.

Among the wagons tied at the hitching rail, Page
spotted a fine horse, travel-stained and well loaded with
handsome saddle bags.

He didn't notice that Red Regan and his crowd had
followed him into the store. "May I post this paper for
the school opening, Mr. Williams?" he asked.

"Sure, Page, put it right up here where everyone can
see it. Now any of you folks want your children to have
book learning, read that. Mr. Carter, here, is going to
open the first school in Serena."

A cotton farmer elbowed his way through the crowd
and read the neat handwriting aloud.

CARTER ACADEMY—SERENA, TEXAS
Oct. 1 to April 1
Reading, writing, arithmetic
geography, history, science
Tuition fee—$5 per month
Cash or Barter
Page Carter, Schoolmaster

"Hey Carter, can you learn anyone to lift a log without dropping it?" Red Regan jeered.

"Or learn them how to kill a turkey?" another boy asked with a meaningful grin.

Miserably Page felt the color come into his face. He didn't see Red Regan's foot shoot out in front of him as he turned to leave. He only felt the hard dirt floor smack his face as he fell. Then for the first time in his life he felt cold hard anger that cried out for sticks, stones, fists, or even a knife if he had one.

Slowly he pushed himself to his knees as the laughing crowd gathered, eager to see a fight. He knew he was one against three, and they all outweighed him.

Before Page could get up, he glimpsed a hard fist jab toward his face. It never landed. A blond giant of a man in buckskins, who had just gotten in to town, caught Red's arm. The crowd was suddenly quiet.

"Let him go, Bowie! Let them fight it out!" a voice demanded.

Bowie, Jim Bowie, thought Page in awe as he struggled to his feet. The man who was famous and feared from Louisiana to Mexico for his duels—and for his knife!

Bowie looked over the crowd with his frosty blue eyes. "I don't mind a good fight. I've had plenty myself. But I don't hold with hitting a man when he's down. And I don't cotton to three against one!"

"You tell them, Jim!" Mr. Williams called from the top of the sugar barrel.

Bowie turned to Page. "You two have some difference to settle?"

"Regan seems to think he has a quarrel with me, sir. I'll fight him, now or later."

A buzz of anticipation ran through the crowd.

Jim Bowie looked from one boy to the other—Red Regan with his broad, hard face and muscles like a panther, Page Carter with the fine-cut features and the tall slight build of a fencer.

"Seems to me, Regan," Bowie drawled, "you're the one who challenged Carter to a fight. In my book, the man who is challenged has the choice of weapons. That's the code. Suit you?"

"Sure," Red bragged. "I can whip him four ways from Sunday."

The big blond man who had fought so many duels glanced out the door at Charcoal. "That your horse, Carter?"

"Yes, sir!" Page answered proudly.

· 100 ·

"Why don't you choose your weapon then—horse racing? Course, one mile."

"I'll take that, Mr. Bowie. Would you be my second, sir?" Page asked eagerly, beginning to see Jim Bowie's plan.

Red Regan scowled. "I don't have no horse that can race."

Bowie released his hand from Red's arm. "You can borrow mine, Regan. Just won a race with him down in San Antone. Pick your own second. We'll make this a real duel. But whoever wins, that's it. You two will shake hands, or else stay away from each other from here on out."

By noon the story was all over town. Excitement ran high in the village where entertainment was scarce. Rumors flew up and down the main street. Marker Wilson was to be second for Red Regan. Judge Anderson would be the time keeper. Mike Dugan would be the starter.

"Page, you must do what you think best, of course," Susan said at dinner, leaving her plate untouched. "But this Jim Bowie—I don't like it. I've heard he's fought a dozen duels that ended in death for others."

"If it hadn't been for Jim Bowie, Mom, I'd have been beaten up by Red and two of his friends. This way it is fair and square." Page grinned as he helped himself to more beans. "I've never had any time to race Charcoal here in Serena. Red probably thinks I can't ride any better than I can shoot or lift logs! I'll win, Mom! Red Regan's too heavy a load for Mr. Bowie's horse to carry."

By two o'clock everyone in Serena had crowded around the finish line just beyond the blacksmith shop. Judge Anderson held his big gold watch in his hand and waited. Susan Carter stood quietly, keeping the anxiety from her eyes.

Page, stripped to the waist, put the light English saddle on Charcoal, carefully adjusted the stirrups and told the little mare just what she must do. "We haven't raced for a long time, but you can still run. You see, the western saddle is heavier. Red Regan is heavier. We travel light, Charcoal. We'll win—we have to win."

As though she understood perfectly, the black mare nuzzled the boy's shoulder and stamped her feet impatiently.

Page trotted down the road to the wagon yard, excited and proud. When he saw Jim Bowie waiting, his confidence grew. It was not everyone who had the famous Mr. Bowie as a "second" in a horse racing duel!

Bowie gravely shook hands with Page. "I'm on your side, son. I never saw you ride, but I've seen other men and horses from Virginia. You have the build—and the horse." He rubbed Charcoal's neck. "But dog me if I see how anyone can stick on a saddle like that!"

"I've never fallen off a horse yet, Mr. Bowie." Page patted his light saddle. "A Texas saddle makes me feel like I'm sitting in a rocking chair!"

Red Regan and Marker Wilson rode up to the starting line. The blacksmith dismounted and came over to inspect Page's horse and saddle while Bowie did the same for Red.

The smith was worried. "Page, how did you let Bowie get you into this?"

"I didn't. Red Regan started the ruckus."

"One minute to go!" bawled Mike Dugan, holding his pistol above his head. Bowie and Marker Wilson stepped back. The sorrel horse Red Regan was riding stepped over the line and was pulled back.

Dugan started to count, one, two. The gun went off with a roar and both horses leaped forward in a smooth stride. Page crouched low over Charcoal's mane as the sorrel kept the pace, neck and neck.

But the day was hot with Indian summer heat. Page pulled the mare in a little and let the sorrel take the lead. Red dug in his heels and pushed the horse to the limit, determined to win by at least two lengths.

Page saw the store flash by. Judge Anderson's flower bed was a blur of color. Now he had passed his own house, the halfway mark. He flattened himself against his horse's neck. "Now, Charcoal," he whispered. "Catch up with him!" His knees gave the signal and the black mare began to gather speed. Slowly Page let her out to run free.

He could see the crowd ahead of him. As he came nearer he could see the sorrel was tiring. Now they were even. Slowly but surely Charcoal pulled ahead, her nostrils wide, ears back in the wind, breathing hard.

The noise of the crowd seemed to act on the black mare like a whip. She was used to wild yelling and noise. With a final sprint she shot across the finish line two lengths ahead of Red Regan on the sorrel.

"Thanks, Charcoal. I knew you could do it. There, old girl, take it easy," Page murmured to the mare, as a dozen hands reached for the bridle and small boys begged for the privilege of rubbing down the winner.

Judge Anderson threw his hat in the air and whooped with delight. Mr. Williams slapped Page on the back. Men he scarcely knew shook hands with him and asked about Charcoal, about the English saddle. Boys his own age wanted to know if he would race them next Saturday. For the first time he felt that he was part of Serena, part of Texas.

When Jim Bowie and Marker Wilson rode up, Page received more congratulations.

"You boys shake hands like I said?" asked Bowie.

"Where's Red?" Page asked.

"There he goes." Marker pointed toward the path into the woods. Red Regan had left Bowie's sorrel tied to a tree. He rode his own sorry nag down the trail without looking back.

The blacksmith's face was stormy. "I'm plumb ashamed of that boy. He's just so all-fired proud, he won't admit he's been whipped fair and square. Well, Jim, at least you tried. I'll have that knife finished tomorrow if you'll come by the shop."

The crowd broke up, still talking about the race. Susan Carter waited, and Page brought Jim Bowie over and introduced him to her.

"It's a pleasure, ma'am. Your son is a credit to you."

"Thank you, Mr. Bowie. If you will accept our hospitality, Page and I would be happy to have you for supper. There's an extra bed in the schoolroom if you'd care to be our guest."

Jim Bowie had meant to visit the doggery and spend the night in the wagon yard with some of his old cronies, but he knew a lady when he met one. "The pleasure is mine, ma'am. I would like to see the Carter Academy. A man who can teach school and win horse races is a rare combination. I think he will have more pupils than he can handle after today!"

It was a merry meal in the Carter cabin that night with Jim Bowie telling tales of New Orleans and San Antone. He seemed to know what a woman liked to hear: how the ladies dressed, and all about the French creole cooking of Louisiana and the chili queens and fiestas of south Texas. Page could see that the handsome, well-mannered man completely won his mother's approval and confidence.

When Susan Carter had gone to bed, Page and Jim Bowie talked of other things before the banked fire in the schoolroom.

· 105 ·

"It takes guts and courage to be a schoolmaster on the frontier, Page." Bowie opened and closed a reader. "I wish I had learned more when I had the chance. But if you are going to live in Texas you'll have to learn to fight, and fight rough."

Page watched the coals drop into ashes. "I have no quarrel with anyone, Mr. Bowie. Why should I fight?"

Bowie's face in the firelight was somber. "There are still Comanches around, son. You have your mother to think about."

"Marker Wilson taught me to shoot. I'm not too good at it—"

"And if you missed and had no time to reload?"

"But I don't have the build or weight for wrestling or fist fighting."

"You could learn to use a knife."

Page shook his head. "I'm just not a born fighter, Mr. Bowie."

Jim Bowie's face tightened stubbornly. "Then you must learn to fight if it means saving your own life. It's not just Indians, Page. Before too long we will be fighting Mexicans."

"Why? The Mexican government gave consent for Stephen Austin to bring in colonists."

"Yes, but now there are more and more Americans coming. They want their own way of life, their own churches, schools and government."

"Surely war will not come here!"

"It's already in the making. With Santa Anna setting up as a dictator, we may have to fight to be free men. I'll teach you to throw a knife. That's something you never have to reload! It's time you learned."

The next morning, in a secluded clearing in the woods, Bowie pulled out a knife and gave it to Page. "That's a duplicate of mine. Marker Wilson did a good job. He's a fine craftsman in metal."

Page looked at the weapon in his hand. It was around ten inches long and at its widest about two inches across. The point had a wicked curve. A fine handle and guard were fashioned to protect the user from cutting his own fingers if his grip slipped.

"Now, watch," Bowie commanded. He drew his knife from his belt with lightning motion and threw it straight into the middle of the knothole which served as a target. "You can tell if it's a good knife because if it is well tempered, it sings when it is thrown."

Page watched closely. "Man named Davy Crockett was in the smithy the other day. He was talking to Marker about your 'Bowie knife.' He said it was 'enough to give a strong man the colic' just to look at it. I can see why!"

Bowie laughed. "Unfortunately, Comanches don't get the colic very easily! Here, you try it. Hold it so—now, throw!" Over and over the knife was thrown. To Page the target seemed to get smaller and smaller. His arm and wrist ached. But he was too proud to call it quits.

They ate their cold lunch and went at it again. By sundown, Page could come nearer the target. He knew what the knife would do, how to carry it, and how to use it. He handed the blade to the man who had taught him. "Thanks, Mr. Bowie. I'll have Marker make me one of those."

Jim Bowie put the knife back in the boy's hand. "This is your knife, Page. Practice every day. When you need it, your knife will sing, like I said. And remember, there comes a time in every man's life when he has to fight, whether he likes it or not. You'll make a good school-master—and a good fighter. *Adios, amigo.*"

Page watched big Jim Bowie ride out of Serena. He wondered if it was true that war would come to the quiet valley of the Brazos.

CHAPTER NINE

Song of the Flute

The yellow and brown fringe of fall draped itself over the Brazos valley in a smoky, golden haze. November had come, and still the days were warm and the winds gentle.

Page sat at his desk in the schoolroom, scarcely blaming the twenty boys in front of him for fidgeting on the hard benches. He would like to be in the wood himself instead of hearing a spelling lesson.

Jim Bowie had been right about filling his schoolroom after the horse race. Boys had flocked in—towheads, redheads and brown heads. Some were from town, some walked several miles from the farms. There were small boys of six. There were some as old as Page. A few knew their letters, but most of them had to start with the alphabet.

Since he had few textbooks, Page had asked every boy to bring a book from home which would serve as a reader. A few had tattered spellers, some had well-marked almanacs, but most of them brought the family Bible, the only book many frontier families owned.

Not all the boys came willingly. A few were sulky, rebelling against enforced learning. Yet, in spite of his doubts, Page had little trouble with discipline. There had been the frog in his desk drawer, the neatly coiled snake in his pencil book, and the water bucket nicely doctored with vinegar. But he didn't mind. He could remember playing the same old tricks on his school-masters.

Now as the afternoon wore on, Page suddenly decided everyone deserved a vacation. He closed his spelling book with a bang and cut Chubby Belton off in the middle of to-bac-co.

"School's out until tomorrow morning," he announced.

The boys whooped with delight. Lunch pails banged. Books were dropped and twenty boys tried to get out the door at one time. Page smiled as he looked at the clutter left behind as the boys boiled down the road into the sunlight yelling for pure joy.

Across the breezeway, Page could hear the chatter of a dozen women as they bent over Susan's quilting frame. Quietly he took his flute from his desk drawer and slipped out the back way. This was not a day he wanted to talk to anyone. He saddled Charcoal for a ride out of town.

Most of the townspeople had been in the original colony of three hundred brought to Texas by Stephen Austin. Under the terms of Austin's agreement with the Mexican government, each had received a land grant which they still used as farm land, raising cotton and corn on farms that ringed the village. Marker Wilson's place lay a mile up the river, where Page supposed Red Regan and his father lived in a shanty of sorts while they picked cotton for the blacksmith. There was the Belton farm, the Williams farm and Judge Anderson's plantation.

Passing them all, Page turned Charcoal off the main road into an unclaimed stretch of woodland half a mile out of town, and down a faint path that led to a heavy thicket with a small clearing in its center. He tied the mare to a post oak and wiggled through a narrow path made by animals, hunters and boys in search of a hideout.

With his back against a water oak, Page sat and looked up at the cloudless blue sky which held no hint of winter. It was warm and still, an almost sullen silence. Even the squirrels failed to chatter. It was as though the land waited for something to come.

Page felt restless and vaguely unhappy. So far, the school had been a success. Although he had taken in only five dollars in actual cash, the Carters now had a milk cow, several pigs and a flock of chickens. There had been hams aplenty, and bacon. Susan had some pretty rag rugs and quilts. Surplus gear or food was traded for staples at Williams' store. Not a dime of hard cash had been spent from their "passage home" money.

So Page knew he had every reason to be satisfied. Yet as a schoolmaster he felt lonely, set apart. When the boys his own age asked him to race or hunt, it was with a certain deference he disliked.

But it's just that I'm not used to summer lasting this long, he thought. When winter comes it will blow these cobwebs out of my head. He took up his flute and put his lips to the cool silver. Softly he played "Come to the Bower" and the few church hymns he had learned for the Sunday service at Judge Anderson's.

Then he began to improvise. He found if he listened closely to the mockingbird, he could repeat the notes on his flute. He could imitate the red bird and the sweet clear notes of the meadowlark. But no birds answered him today. Even the noisy blue jays were quiet.

He had no idea how long he had been playing when he had the strange feeling he was not alone. Uneasily, he put down the flute and looked about. There was nothing to see, nothing to hear, but he was mortally certain he was being watched. Probably some of his pupils were waiting to toll him into some trap. He grinned and waited, pretending to be asleep.

But no rowdy little boys crept up on him. The silence

grew. Finally, he could stand it no longer. Taking the flute, he started to get up. Then a warm, copper-colored hand flicked from behind the tree and pushed him down. From right and left came two more Indians.

He was surprised. The fear came later. He had never before seen an Indian. These were big and greasy, clad only in breech clout and moccasins. The braided black hair, high cheekbones, and scarred faces frightened Page as much as the array of knives and arrows.

His mind circled. He had no gun. It was too late to pull his Bowie knife. Charcoal was hidden in the thicket. She would make her way home if he were killed.

In Serena he had heard many tales of Indian cruelties. He only hoped his end would be quick. Yet nothing happened. He realized the leader of the group was not looking at him but at the flute on the ground.

So that was it. They had heard him playing. Quickly he picked up the pipe and once more put it to his lips. The big brave with the red feather in his hair nodded. Page felt his breath stick in his chest. But somehow he blew a few notes. The brave shook his head.

After several other false tries, he stumbled onto the mockingbird notes he had made up. The red feathered Comanche nodded his head. He made motions to his comrades. One of them seized the flute. The other one grabbed Page by the hair and drew his knife.

But the brave shouted a few angry words and Page was released. Now the Indian took the flute and put

it to his thick lips. No sound came out. He shook it furiously, and tried it again.

Page was certain he wasn't going to live anyway, but he decided to take a chance. He got up and motioned to the Comanche, making signs with his fingers as though playing the flute.

Finally the flute was handed back. With very slow motion, Page showed how he placed his fingers over the holes in the pipe, then raising them as he blew. He gave the flute back to the redskin who tried, but failed again.

With sign language and with the flute, he finally made Page understand what he wanted—"Teach me to play the bird notes, and you can go home." He ordered the others to be on their way.

How did you teach an Indian whose language you did not know? What if he couldn't learn? You just have to get your head up and travel on. That was what Marker Wilson had said.

He motioned to the Comanche to sit by his side and watch. Then he repeated over and over the lip and finger movements. The warrior sat silently, watching. Again and again he tried. Now Page had courage enough to move the copper hands to the right position. He could feel sweat running down his back.

The sky became leaden and the shadows deepened as still the big Comanche tried. Page could see that the man was becoming angry. He knew the Indian thought the flute had been commanded not to play for him.

If only the man would blow softly, not with such a rush of air from his big chest. In desperation, Page took up a leaf and blew hard until it waved frantically. Then he shook his head at the brave. Now he blew very softly until the leaf barely quivered and nodded his head in approval.

Once again the flute changed hands and the copper fingers closed over the holes. Softly the Comanche breathed into the pipe. A wild note came out, clear and strong. Page never had heard a sweeter sound. The Comanche was delighted. He had learned. He raised one finger then another. A strange music filled the air. It was enough to frighten even a raucous blue jay. But the brave was satisfied. He got up and made signs to the boy to go.

Taking a last look at the silver flute, Page started out of the clearing, wondering at each step if an arrow or knife would stop him. But the Comanche seemed unaware of his going. He blew again and again upon the wonderful new thing that was his, a thing which answered the birds.

When he reached Charcoal, Page was trembling with exhaustion and fright. Controlling his urge to break into a hard gallop, he held the horse to a steady canter and rode to the smithy where Marker Wilson was closing his shop for the night.

"Page," Marker shouted, "what's the matter? White as a rabbit's hide you are, boy!"

Page slipped from his horse and ran into the cabin. "Indians! They got my flute, but they let me go. They might come tonight and mother is alone. I have to get on!"

Marker could scarcely believe his ears. "Where, son? You sure you haven't got the chills and fever?" To make certain, he dashed a gourd of water in the boy's face.

Page pulled himself together and told his story. "Warn the others, Marker. I have to get home."

The smith threw his saddle on the bay and picked up both his guns. "I'll go with you. Don't frighten your ma. Just say I come to supper. Then I'll sleep in the schoolroom without her knowing. If there were only three Comanches, I doubt they'd come to town except to steal horses. But mebbe there were more in the woods."

Marker dropped Page off at his cabin and cantered on down the road to spread the alarm. When he came back and sat down at the table with a hearty appetite, Page wondered if he had dreamed the whole episode. But his flute was gone.

The boy ate little but Marker outdid himself, complimented Susan on the stew, the new quilt, and casually examined the gun given in barter for tuition. "This lock needs a mite of straightening, Page. Barrel don't seem quite true either." With that excuse he took the rifle with him.

After he left, Susan went peacefully to bed, quite

unaware that in the schoolroom across the breezeway, Marker Wilson sat with three loaded guns. As soon as his mother was asleep, Page joined him, carrying his own rifle, ammunition and Bowie knife.

Marker quietly chained Charcoal and his own bay outside the window. "There's two horses they won't get," he told Page, as he warmed his hands in front of the fire. "Don't think they'll strike tonight, though. Norther coming in."

"Norther?"

"Land almighty, boy! Didn't you see that sulky sky come up in the north this afternoon. Everything as still as a graveyard. Always like that just before a blue norther strikes. Wind shifted to the north while I was chaining up the horses just now."

Page shivered and put another log on the fire. "Sure is getting cold. Why, just a few hours ago it was warm like summer."

"Well, it'll drop thirty degrees in the next hour and I'll wager those Indians are huddled around a fire somewhere, just like the folks in Serena. But we got the sentries out anyway. Can't afford to take a chance."

"How do they give the alarm if there's a real raid?" Page asked anxiously, straining his hears to hear above the howl of the wind.

Marker pulled his bench closer to the fire. "Just ride hell-bent-for-leather up the main street yelling! Sure wish we had us a big bell to ring. I got the iron saved to make one, but there's no way to cast a bell so far away from a foundry."

Page put another quilt around his shoulders, and studied the flames, his mind reaching back to an almost forgotten history book in the Richmond academy. Somewhere he had read about the making of bells long before there had been the process of casting.

"I remember now, Marker," he said. "You could make a bell. It wouldn't have the tone of a real shaped bell, but it could be heard all over town if it were needed. Long years ago in Europe, men made bells by soldering or riveting four pieces of metal together to form a rectangular bell."

The smith cocked his ear as the wind slapped a tree branch against the cabin wall. "I've seen cow bells made that way, but never did think of making a big one. Sure would make a noise, though. Better than nothing. Beats me how you can remember all those things you read in books!"

As the night wore on they took turns dozing by the fire. When the first cock crowed, Marker woke the boy and stole out of the schoolroom. Page slipped back to the other cabin and was sound asleep when Susan put the coffee pot on the fire.

Knowing the danger was over, at least for the time being, Page told her the story of the Comanches and the flute and of the long night watch. "I'm sorry about father's flute, Mom."

"If you hadn't had the flute to give, Page, you might not be here now. After all, you still have the fife you could play." Susan tried not to show her concern.

"Marker says now that the norther has come, the Indians will go back to their fires," he told her. "Just keep the door barred and the latchstring in."

Gradually the vigilance of the village was relaxed. Attendance at school came back to normal. Thanksgiving came and went with bountiful feasting. Page brought out his father's fife and through the long evenings tried to play it as he had the flute. But the tones were shrill. The sound was not the same.

One day he put on his heavy blanket coat and coonskin cap and headed for the smithy. Maybe Marker had the bell done by now. He had been working on it for several weeks, determined to provide some sort of alarm for Serena.

But Page found Marker saddled and ready to ride. "Man from upriver in here this morning. Said some horses had been stolen. Thought I'd go out to my farm and see how Red and his pa were making out." He patted the tow sack back of his saddle. "Always take a little coffee and meal. Want to come along?"

Page had no desire to see either Red Regan or his pa, but he remembered the threatening faces of the Comanches. He did not want Marker to go alone.

They cantered down the road rutted by the early

freeze, rifles on the pommels of their saddles, their eyes searching the tangled thickets.

After a silent mile, they turned into the clearing humped with tree stumps where a rough shack leaned against a big live oak. Marker called loudly, but there was no answer. "Red's horse isn't here. Guess they must be out chopping firewood."

Page rode behind Marker into the cleared fields where the old cotton stalks were brown and brittle. Still there was no sign of life. "Might be down at the river fishing," Page suggested.

They turned their horses and went back to the river, pulling up on the steep bank to listen. Marker's sharp eyes looked anxiously now for sign. Suddenly, he slipped from his saddle. "Been trouble here. Keep me covered." He crawled down the incline toward the water, moving quietly through the heavy tangle of vines and underbrush.

There was silence except for the murmur of the river. Page could feel his hands stiffen on the reins.

"Bring the horses down!" Marker called softly.

Page urged Charcoal down the embankment. Marker was kneeling over something in the grass. A man lay face up on the muddy ground, his eyes unseeing, an arrow through his chest. It was Pa Regan.

Page felt sick. They looked in vain for Red. "Like as not he saw it happen and ran for the woods. They must have got Pa last night. Could be Red is in Serena by now," Marker said hopefully. They took Pa Regan back to town.

Marker insisted Pa must rest in the Serena burial ground, no matter what many folks said. But Judge Anderson, who always preached the funerals, was out of town. The next morning, cold and raw with a light rain falling, only a few stood around the coffin Marker had made. Red was not there. After Susan Carter read from the Bible, Marker Wilson bowed his big head in the chilling mist.

"Lord," he said softly, "Pa Regan wasn't much, but please do what you can for him. He had a rough time and he died hard. In a manner of speaking, he was one of us. Amen."

CHAPTER TEN

Indian Raid

For several weeks the men of Serena went about their business with rifles handy. Heavy doors were barred at night, and horses were staked out near the cabins. The village looked peaceful enough with the blue smoke curling from the cabin chimneys, but men no longer went into the woods alone to cut wood or hunt for game.

Even in the schoolroom, rifles were stacked near the door. Every boy over twelve brought his own gun. Those who came from the farms and plantations were boarded with friends or relatives in town.

Page went on with the lessons but he knew that today of all days there would be little learned. Marker Wilson had passed the word that the new bell would be tried out at two o'clock. Everyone had been asked to stay home with doors and windows barred to see if the alarm could be heard.

At half past one, Page turned the school over to his mother, and rode eagerly to the smithy. The town seemed deserted, shut up and still. Judge Anderson and Marker were waiting, looking up anxiously at the big rectangular bell which hung above the blacksmith shop.

The judge repeated the plan posted in Williams' store. "Continued ringing means bar the doors, load your guns and stay where you are. One short clang says all men come to the smithy. Two short clangs means go to Williams' store. Extra arms are stacked in each place."

"Everyone will remember the signals," Marker said, "if the bell can just be heard far enough."

The judge put the rawhide rope in Page's hand. "You're the one had the idea for the bell, son. You give the first signal." He looked at his big gold watch and nodded.

Page pulled again and again on the rope as the mighty clang echoed through the village. Marker gave the short ring and Judge Anderson rang twice. Then people came pouring out of their cabins, happy that the new alarm had worked.

Mustang Brown who lived in the last cabin to the north came running down the road, his beard streaming in the wind, his eyes wild with fright. "Give me a gun," he shouted. "Let's go get 'em!"

Marker doubled up with laughter. "Guess you forget we were only trying out the bell today! Look like a bear took after you."

"Danged if I didn't forget it," Mustang said sheepishly. "That thing rattled my teeth so hard I choked on my cornbread while I was eating dinner!"

Marker looked up proudly at the bell. "I reckon not a soul in town but can hear that racket. But someday, I'm gonna have me a real pretty sounding church bell."

When everyone had gone home, Page went in for a cup of coffee with Marker. "Heard anything about Red Regan?"

The smith's big face darkened. "No. I asked the Captain of the *Yellowstone* if he saw him in Galveston, but he never did. Could be he joined up with Sam Houston's army. General Houston asked for volunteers, you know."

"Looks like we're having enough Indian trouble without having to fight Mexicans too. I don't like it, Marker."

The smith poured himself some more coffee. "Lots of folks don't like it, son, but like Jim Bowie said, the fight is going to come, like it or not."

As the bleak December wore on, the Indian scare died down. Latchstrings were left out again and the Comanches were almost forgotten in the talk that swept up and down the river from San Felipe to Serena to Washington-on-the-Brazos.

A meeting was called in the schoolroom and Judge Anderson tried to sift fact from rumor and explain what was going on. "As you know," he said, "Mexico allowed Stephen Austin to bring three hundred American families to Texas. Some of you were among them. Those families were promised protection as well as land and certain liberties."

"We never got no protection from the Comanches," shouted a farmer whose cabin had been burned several years before by Indians.

"That's just the point, gentlemen. The Mexican government has not fulfilled its promise. Furthermore, as more Americans come to Texas, Mexico likes it less and less. Santa Anna stands for oppression, even of his own people."

Mike Dugan spoke up. "I say we oughta fight. After all, Judge, you went to the meeting down to San Felipe when they wrote that paper asking real polite to be a state and have their own government. And Austin took it down to Mexico City to this Santa Anna and ends up in the jailhouse."

The judge looked grave. "Yes, that is quite true. Austin was double crossed. Santa Anna listened to his request and pretended to agree. He let him start home, then had him arrested and thrown in a dungeon, along with Mexicans who stood for liberty."

"I don't aim to jump into a fight," Marker said slowly. "But when Santa Anna's men sent soldiers to Gonzales to take back a cannon they had given those folks to keep off the Indians, I don't blame the men of the town for getting riled."

"What happened?" asked a settler who had just arrived from the States.

"Why," Marker told him, "the Gonzales men buried the cannon in a peach orchard and put up a flag that read 'come and take it.' They dug up that cannon, filled it full of nails, horse shoes and scrap iron and fired it at the Mexicans."

Page sat quietly listening to the news of the seizure of guns at the Mexican arms depot in Goliad. He heard about the march on San Antonio held by the Mexican General Cos.

"Us Texans sure whipped ole Cos," Mike Dugan said gleefully.

Judge Anderson sighed. "Yes, three hundred men defeated General Cos and his fourteen hundred men. But the Mexicans are not whipped. I'm afraid I agree with General Houston, head of the Texas army. We've won a few battles because the Mexicans were unprepared. But wars are never won by untrained and undisciplined armies. The big fight is yet to come. Santa Anna is bound to seek revenge for those defeats."

"Is it true," Page asked, "that some of the men are talking about invading Mexico?"

"Yes, it is," Marker answered shortly. "But I agree with the judge and with Sam Houston. We don't want Mexico. We just want Texas. Give some folks a taste of winning and they get too big for their britches!"

"Time will tell, Marker," the judge said. "Some of the men from Serena have already rushed off to join the army."

"Anyone come back who might have seen Red Regan in the army?" Marker asked hopefully.

"I saw a wagon master back from Goliad," Belton said, "but he didn't remember any redhead. Quit worrying, Marker. That young'un has nine lives."

Christmas came and went in Serena as it did elsewhere. Fathers sat up late at night whittling whistles and toys. Mothers fashioned rude cornshuck dolls by candlelight, and brought out precious scraps of ribbon and paper for decorations.

Boys swarmed through the wood to gather wild growing holly. Chubby Belton fell out of a tree gathering mistletoe and had his broken wrist set by the blacksmith. Mr. Williams hoarded a supply of rock candy that came all the way from New Orleans.

Parents crowded into the schoolroom to hear the Christmas program and sing carols. The fiddle twanged and Page's fife played softly while Susan Carter sang "Come to the Bower," and "God Rest you Merry Gentlemen" floated out into the crisp night air.

But underneath it all Page knew there was little rest and none of the gentlemen were very merry. Another farmer had seen Indian sign and his horses were stolen. Judge Anderson looked troubled when he had come back from a meeting in San Felipe, reporting only dis-agreement and bitter words among the leaders of the Texas colony.

Page sat long in front of the fire that night when all the guests had gone. His mind was far away in Virginia. He remembered the celebration at the academy and the music in the church, followed by cake and punch at home. He hadn't seen white bread or cake for six months. He remembered shouts of "Christmas gift!" echoing through the little brick house. He could almost hear his father playing the silver flute when friends dropped by for eggnog.

"Page, it was a nice school program. All the parents were so proud and pleased!" Susan Carter put her sewing away and ruffled her son's hair as she passed. "Do you mind Texas too much?"

Page was ashamed of his own unhappiness. His mother never complained about things she missed, friends she had left, fear of the future. "No, Mom, I just keep thinking you should have a new bonnet."

Susan laughed. "There's not a woman in Serena has a new bonnet!"

Page grinned and pulled a box from under his bed. "Then you'll be the first, Mom. I sent to New Orleans for this one—one like Mr. Bowie talked about. Merry Christmas!"

The sight of his mother parading about the rough cabin in her homespun dress with a New Orleans bonnet made Page realize all the fun had not gone out of the world. And he knew proudly that she would be the envy of every woman in town.

Then Susan brought her gift from hiding—a shiny new pair of boots big enough for Page's ever-growing feet. The boy pulled them on, happy to discard his old ones. But as he felt their softness he wondered how long they would last tramping the muddy road with an army.

January was cold and dismal. Page could not get his schoolboys down to the business of learning the multiplication table, for they were too restless. Some of their fathers were already with the scattered forces of the Texas army. Grim-faced men from the hills of Tennessee and Kentucky passed through town on their way to join Sam Houston.

Page decided that a spelling match might liven up the dull day and started to close the arithmetic book. Suddenly the dread sound of the bell at the smithy cut through the room, with one sharp clang.

The cabin was in a turmoil as boys ran for their stacked rifles, pulling on coats and coonskin caps, yelling and fighting to get out first.

Page reached over their heads and barred the door. "Now listen to me," he said sternly. "I'm needed at the smithy. All boys over twelve with rifles step to this side." Immediately all the pupils from six years up moved to the side indicated.

Susan came bursting in the door, her face white.

"Here's the other gun, Page. Hurry! I'll stay with the smaller ones. Leave the pistol for me."

Page quickly separated the boys under twelve and sent them to the other cabin with his mother. Five boys grabbed their rifles and raced to the smithy on their horses, with Page setting the pace.

Marker was looking anxiously down the road. "Where is everyone, boy?"

Judge Anderson galloped up on his fast sorrel. "Everyone but us went south to get that wagon train through three hours ago. Said they expected Indian trouble."

The blacksmith clapped his fur cap on his head and pointed to the back of the shop. A man with an arrow in his back lay face down. "Mustang Brown. He made it to the shop and fell over. Comanches raided his farm a mile out and got all of his horses. He was alone and lit out for town. Got him in the back."

Judge Anderson's face was set as he looked over his "army." One blacksmith, one schoolmaster, one lawyer, and five boys from twelve to fifteen who had never seen an Indian in their lives.

"You boys sure you want to go? This is not a play party."

Chubby Belton brandished his gun. "I can shoot, Judge, honest I can. I could kill five Indians!"

Judge Anderson turned his horse. "No firing unless I give the word. Just a show of force might run them off.

Stay together and keep quiet. Marker, you take advance scout. Page, you take rear guard."

They rode down the frozen road with no sound except the creak of saddle leather and the clop of a steady canter.

Cautiously, they cleared the woods that surrounded Brown's cotton farm. The cabin was still smoking. The Comanches had burned everything. Page was thankful Brown had neither wife nor child.

The judge eyed the ruin. "They've run off that herd of mustangs Brown spent so many months breaking. Can you read sign, Marker?"

Marker nodded grimly and rode on toward the north, his sharp eyes scanning the ground as he followed a trail even Page could identify.

"How many were there?" Chubby whispered, as he crowded his horse close to Marker.

"About six or eight, boy. You get back where you belong."

They swung away from the river now toward the high prairie to the west. Here there were few trees on the rolling plain covered with knee high brown grass.

Marker signaled a halt. "They're in that ravine up ahead if I know those Comanches," he said quietly. "If we charge down on them, they've got the advantage of shooting arrows over the edge of that cut without us seeing where to fire."

The judge looked at the boys and then at the blacksmith. "I think it would be better if we tricked them. Right here at the edge of this grove of trees, let's make a barricade of our saddles. Then we'll let two of the boys ride out a few yards on the prairie. The Indians see them and think they are alone. The boys ride back into the grove. The Comanches will boil out of that ravine after them and we'll meet them with a steady line of fire."

Marker nodded. He motioned to the two twelve-year-old boys whose ruddy cheeks had become a little pale. "You two ride out as far as that sapling. Stop and pretend to look all around. Then turn your horses and ride back slowly. Soon as you hit the trees, dismount and get on your bellies back of the barricade. Here, give me your rifles."

Page could see the boys grip their reins until their fingers were white. He edged Charcoal between their horses. "Look, you're out of range of their arrows all the way out and back. Just say the multiplication tables up to nine times eight and you'll be back before you know it!"

Marker kept the two riders covered while the judge and Page built up the saddle barricade, checked all the guns, and turned the horses over to Chubby. "Take them farther back in the woods and tie them. Stay right there until you're needed."

Now the two boys were riding back. Quickly they slipped from their saddles and threw themselves behind the barricade. The judge at one end of the line laid two pistols and a rifle within reach. Marker took the other end of the line and Page took the middle, feeling in his belt for the knife Jim Bowie had said would sing.

He knew what the boys on either side of him were feeling. His own mouth was dry, too. "Wait until you can see what to hit," he cautioned. "And keep your heads down."

"Here they come," whispered Marker. "Hold your fire."

Up from the ravine came six Comanches, riding arrogantly across the plain, bows at the ready, their buckskin breeches black with grime, their faces bare of war paint.

"It's not a war party, just a bunch of horse thieves," said the judge.

On the redskins came at a steady lope until Page could feel his teeth gritting as he sighted down the long rifle barrel. Just as the first Indian reached over his shoulder for an arrow from his quiver, Judge Anderson signaled with raised thumb—fire!

The sudden ripple of flame came as a surprise to the Indians. One horse went down. A Comanche toppled from his saddle as the others wheeled, leaving only a few scattered arrows in front of the barricade.

Page was thankful Marker had taught him to reload quickly, for again the Comanches galloped toward them, yelling savagely, angry at being tricked. Another volley, ragged though it was, turned them back.

Marker let out his breath. "They won't come again. Let's get our horses and run them off. The herd is there somewhere."

As they turned toward the wood, a horse and rider shot through their line and dashed after the retreating Comanches.

"Chubby," roared Marker, "come back here!" But Chubby Belton was yelling in triumph as he rode. The Comanche leader, with a red feather in his hair, turned and saw his pursuer. Calmly he fitted an arrow to his bow and let it fly. Chubby fell from his horse into the dry grass.

Judge Anderson stood up, took careful aim and fired. The red-feathered Indian pitched forward and fell. The other five warriors disappeared into the ravine.

Page scrambled over the saddles and ran onto the prairie, grabbed Chubby by his deerhide belt and pulled him back to the barricade where Marker hoisted him to safety.

"Fool thing to do," he grunted at Page. "Get yourself killed."

Chubby opened his eyes. "It hurts," he moaned.

Marker looked at the arrow which had gone through the boy's arm. "It will hurt worse when I take it out! Here, chew down hard on this." He stuffed the boy's mouth with his own belt, broke off the arrow head and pulled it out.

With a piece of Judge Anderson's shirt, Page bound

up the wound. "Fighting is just like school, Chubby," he said gently. "First thing you have to learn is discipline."

One of the other boys brought up the horses. "Look," Marker pointed to the prairie. "Here comes one of those Comanches waving something white."

"He wants the body of that Indian," the judge said. "They never leave their dead. Let's bargain for the horses. I'll go out to meet him."

Marker shoved the judge behind the saddles. "I savvy a little Comanche. I'll take care of the pow-wow. But keep me covered."

The smith climbed over the barricade and walked slowly to meet the Indian beside the body of the Comanche leader. Page could see them exchanging words and sign language. Then Marker stooped and looked at something. "Page," he called. "Come here— unarmed!"

Page ran to the blacksmith. Then he saw it, his silver flute, stuck in the dead Comanche's belt. He stooped to pick it up, but the Indian with the white rag protested violently.

"Let it be," Marker ordered.

The conference went on in strange words Page could not understand. Finally Marker turned to the boy. "He says we can have the horses if we let them have the body."

"Fine!" Page exclaimed. "All I want is my flute."

"That's just it, Page," the blacksmith explained. "They want the flute to bury with the body. When a Comanche dies, they believe he will never go to the happy hunting ground unless he is buried with everything he needs. This warrior apparently needs your flute to wake the birds every morning. That's what this jasper says, anyway!"

"But Marker, I can't—"

The Indian broke into angry words again. Marker looked surprised, then highly excited as he translated to Page. "He says they must have the flute. If you let him have it, they will return to us a white prisoner they have!"

The happiness Page had felt when he saw the flute was gone now. But in its place came warmth of feeling he had never known. He could buy a man's life for a silver flute! "Of course, Marker. Tell him they can have the flute, but make him bring the prisoner here and release him first."

Marker sent the man on his way and turned to Page. "I'm sorry, son. I know that flute belonged to your pa and his pa before him. But being a Comanche prisoner— well, I know. I was captured once."

Both of them strained their eyes as the Indian rode back from the ravine leading the captive by a rope. He was white, they could see that now. He was thin and shuffled along like a dazed animal. Now they could see his stone-cut feet, his ragged buckskins, his gaunt face.

The prisoner was Red Regan.

CHAPTER ELEVEN

The Runaway Scrape

For several weeks Red Regan lay ill in the blacksmith's cabin. Fever made him babble endlessly of hunger and cold and a mother he had known long ago.

When he was up again he did not seem like the same boy. He was quiet and said little. As he grew stronger, he pulled bellows for Marker Wilson and cared for the horses left over night.

Page, busy with his schoolroom, didn't see Red until he took Charcoal to the smithy to be shod. Marker had gone to the wharf to meet the *Yellowstone*.

Page tried to be friendly. "Glad you're feeling better, Red."

Regan pretended to be busy sorting nails. "I guess if you'd knowed it was me, you wouldn't have give up your fancy flute."

"A flute is little enough to give for a life. Anyone would have done the same."

"I'll buy you another flute," Red muttered as he saw Marker ride up.

"There's no need, Red. I still have my fife." Page knew the boy could not bring himself to say thanks, that he still felt like an outcast in Serena. Better to keep away, Page decided. If my life had been saved by someone I disliked, I'd feel the same way.

After that, he avoided the smithy as much as possible. He had no time for loafing, for there was school to keep, and with the growing warmth of the early spring, a garden to make and tend.

Nor was he just a schoolmaster. As unrest grew in Texas, white-topped wagons began to come through Serena headed not west, but east. Many families were leaving Texas.

"You can't just feed these people and bed them down as though they were guests, Page," the judge pointed out. "We might as well face it. That Mexican general is out for revenge. Santa Anna may sweep clear across Texas unless Sam Houston and his small army can stop him. Lots of folks don't have much faith in our government or our army. They're leaving."

"You're staying?" Page asked.

"Yes, I'm staying. This is my home and my country. Now put up a sign 'Carter Inn' and let everyone pay regular prices if they're so anxious to get across the

Brazos. They'll move out every morning early enough for you to hold school."

Page took the judge's advice and put up his sign. By the end of February there was never a night that the beds were not filled and the schoolroom full of sleeping men rolled in blankets. It was not easy, running both a school and hotel, but with every silver dollar he added to the "passage money home," his spirits rose. Another few weeks and he would have two hundred and fifty dollars.

On March 3, the bell at the smithy sounded once. But Page knew it was no Indian warning. A town meeting had been called by Judge Anderson, who had just come back from San Felipe where the future of Texas was in the making.

In half an hour, every man in the village was there, standing or hunkering on his heels around the warmth of the fire. Voices were raised in argument.

Marker Wilson brought down his big hammer for order. Judge Anderson, his face grave and tired, his boots caked with mud, took his place behind the forge.

"Gentlemen," he said quietly. "The die has been cast. Yesterday the fifty-nine delegates to the convention in San Felipe declared Texas independent of Mexico. A constitution insuring every man's right to live and worship as he pleases has been written and signed. Your president is Mr. David Burnet. The commander-in-chief of the Texas army is Sam Houston."

Heavy feet stomped on the hard dirt flood in approval.

"When is Houston gonna fight ole Santa Anny?" yelled Mike Dugan.

"When you get there to lead the attack, Dugan!" one of his friends replied, and cheers rose to the rafters.

Marker pounded for silence. The judge looked over the crowd. Men with children. Men with sons old enough to fight. Men with farms and men with businesses in Serena.

"Houston has asked for volunteers. Some have already gone from here. But the real fight has not yet come. Let us not be too hasty. Let Houston organize his force, then we will be ready to join him."

The next week was full of talk and wild rumors. Men gathered at Williams' store to discuss their new independence. Where was the army? How many men had joined up?

They met in Mike Dugan's doggery. Where was Santa Anna with his Mexicans? Had reinforcements reached the beleagured Alamo in San Antonio, where Jim Bowie and a handful of men were holding out against Santa Anna's forces in a desperate siege?

Page found himself sorely troubled. When Marker dropped in with a bag of rabbits for supper, Page was glad Susan had gone to a quilting party. He wanted to talk to the blacksmith alone.

"I have enough money to leave for Virginia, Marker," he told him. "The lock box has two hundred and fifty dollars in hard money. The *Yellowstone* docks next week."

Marker poked up the fire. "Your ma anxious to go, son?"

"She's going to be surprised. She's waited so long. And she has no idea we've earned so much running Carter Inn! She'll be happy again, in Virginia."

"Reckon she will," Marker agreed without enthusiasm. "Sorry to see you leave, boy. We've got lots to do here in Texas."

Page could sense the big man's disappointment. "Marker," Page said, "this isn't my fight. I've only been here nine months."

"I reckon you're right. But you better get out pretty quick. Things aren't going too good with Houston's army. Seems like everyone wants him to fight right now. But I know Big Sam. When he's good and ready he'll fight. Bunch of deserters drifted through here today. I told them to just keep going."

Page was so rapt in his dream of Virginia that he paid little heed to the increasing number of wagons being ferried across the Brazos to the road that led east out of Texas. He was busy making plans. Tomorrow he would book passage for two on the *Yellowstone,* due to leave Serena April 1.

In a week now they could put the cabin up for sale and get a good price for the wagon which still stood at the back of the lot. Mr. Belton had said folks would pay real money for a wagon nowadays.

It was a balmy day in mid-March when Page saw from the school window a dust-covered man streak down the road on a horse flecked with foam. Then Marker's bell began to ring—not a sharp clang, but a slow toll.

People started to stream down the road toward the smithy. Page dismissed school and hurried with the others to the blacksmith shop. The rider, now on a fresh horse, was just disappearing toward Washington-on-the Brazos.

Marker left a horse half shod and turned to the crowd. "The Alamo has fallen. Every man was butchered. Their bodies were burned. Less'n two hundred men held out six days against a Mexican army of four thousand. They could have left, but they stayed. Some of our best men—Fannin, Travis, Crockett and Bowie."

The crowd dispersed, talking in low tones among themselves, their hearts heavy. Page went to Marker and put his hand on the smith's shoulder. "Bowie was your friend, I know. He was my friend, too."

Red Regan blew up the fire. "I rode Jim Bowie's horse once. I ain't never forgot him letting me ride that horse when I didn't have nothing but a sorry old nag."

Page found it hard to sleep that night. He finally took his fife and walked out on the prairie under the stars wheeling slowly in the grey blue sky. He wondered what the men at the Alamo had thought as they watched the same stars for the last time, knowing the attack would come at dawn.

He tried to think about the coming trip to Virginia, but it was Jim Bowie who strode across his mind. Jim Bowie with the wide grin and the quick knife-hand. He heard him saying again, "I don't hold with three against one. It's got to be fair and square."

Well, it wasn't that way at the Alamo, Page thought. He remembered the other words. "Comes a time when a man has to fight whether he likes it or not."

Page walked slowly back and forth in the crisp night that was half spring. He tried to put together the things he knew. His grandfather had been at Valley Forge with Washington, but the old man had never liked to talk about it. "Never forget, boy, wars are not for glory or fame. War is wretched business. But what you're fighting for is the thing that matters. Men will find out from here to eternity that 'freedom is a hard bought thing'."

Yes, he knew his grandfather had fought for freedom even though he had been in the colonies just a few years. Page tried to persuade himself that his own case was different. But he realized it was not. He owed it to Serena to stay. He owed it to Marker, and he owed it to Jim Bowie.

The next day Page waited until the last sum was done, the last word spelled in the lesson. Then he closed his books and looked at the boys squirming on the hard benches. "This is the last day of school," he said slowly.

"I hope you will remember what you have learned. Help your families in the hard days to come. I am going to join Sam Houston's army."

The boys crowded about, begging to go with him, but Page sent them home and went to find Marker. "Here's my gun. I wish you would mend this lock. I'll send my mother to Virginia, but I'm staying to fight."

"I kinda thought you would, son. Leave the rifle. I'll get it done."

Page looked at the guns stacked along the wall, all needing repair. A dozen horses stamped impatiently waiting to be shod.

Red Regan looked up from the forge. "I aim to go to the army tomorrow."

"You're not going anywheres 'til we get all these guns and horses ready," Marker snapped. "Your ma know, Page?"

That was the question. Page dreaded telling his mother the decision he had made.

But Susan Carter was not surprised. "I knew you would feel you must go, Page. I can manage here."

"Mother, you must go on to Virginia. We have the money."

"No. This is my home, now." They argued far into the night, but Susan Carter refused to go.

Nor did Page leave the next day. The news came that Sam Houston was retreating toward the Brazos. Gonzales had been put to the torch by the Mexicans. Many

Texans had been killed at Goliad.

Refugees poured into Serena. They came by ox cart, by covered wagon, on mud-spattered horses, and on foot. Day after day they streamed down the road, made into a quagmire by the spring rains. The Brazos was rising rapidly. The ferry plied back and forth across the ugly red torrent, with every man aboard poling desperately to keep the light raft on its course.

Many of the wagons held only women and tired, crying children. Page heard the squawking of cooped hens, the bawling of a cow dragged behind a tailboard. And always the frenzied cracking of a whip, and the impatient voices of men pushing their horses too long and too far. If the wagons bogged down in the mud, they had to sit and wait for help. Some lightened their loads by leaving behind precious furniture or food.

Page scarcely knew day from night. He organized his schoolboys into teams, putting their shoulders to mud-bound wheels, or passing out hot cornbread and coffee which Susan made.

The roads were jammed. The river rose higher. The spring rains beat down. From the west came news that Sam Houston was retreating further toward the Brazos. The Mexican army in pursuit left fire, death and destruction in its wake.

Marker came to the Carter cabin just before dusk, his face drawn with weariness and worry. "Page, we've got to get your mother and all the others in town across the river and on the way to Nacogdoches. Houston's army is just a mile south of Serena. He means to cross the river here. The Mexicans will arrive in a few days."

"We can't let the women go alone, Marker."

"They won't be alone. Judge Anderson is just getting over malaria. He's in no shape to go traipsin' around with an army. He'll drive the women folks to safety. Just a good thing you never sold that wagon. Get packed up."

Page felt numb. Surely this couldn't be happening to Serena. But Susan Carter had heard what the smith had said. "Come on, Page," she ordered briskly. "Get the lantern lighted. We're going to bury the silver, china and books. Wrap them well in quilts."

All that night the two of them worked, digging trenches, putting in their treasures, replacing the green sod, and marking down the locations.

By early morning the wagon was loaded. Page looked around the cabin at the desk, the fourposter, the fine chest and delicate chairs. "You could put some of these in, Mom. There's room."

"No," Susan spoke firmly. "I've seen too many wagons bog down from overloading. There are the very old and young to be picked up along the way. Food and bedding are more important than furniture."

Page put out the fire, gathered up his rifle, ammunition and his fife, then barred the doors and windows. Marker had already hitched up the team. Judge Anderson was

on the wagon seat. Inside were Miss Williams, Mrs. Belton with Chubby and his dog, Kentucky, Mrs. Dugan, and Susan Carter.

Mounting Charcoal, Page joined Marker Wilson to escort the wagon across the river. Red Regan pulled up on the judge's sorrel which he was to take across on the ferry.

Slowly they inched their way onto the road that was already choked with wagons and carts. The ferryman swore he could not get across the rising river one more time. The nine hundred tired and discouraged men of Sam Houston's army stretched a mile down the road from the wharf.

Marker rode back and forth relaying messages and news, trying to quell the panic that was fast gripping the families which had sat for hours in motionless wagons.

"No ma'am," he answered one hysterical woman. "Sam Houston says not one soldier goes across until all the refugees are on the other side."

Off he rode again only to come back with more important news. "Sam Houston has commandeered the *Yellowstone* tied up at the wharf. Soon as everyone leaves town, the army can get across on that. The decks are barricaded with cotton bales in case Santa Anna gets here to fight before they can make it!"

Page could feel the tension mounting as he rode up and down the line of wagons all inching slowly toward the river. It was almost dusk when the Carter wagon slid down the cutbank and onto the ferry.

"Hurry up," yelled the ferryman. "This is the last trip!"

Just then Chubby's dog bounded from the wagon and started up the bank. Chubby ran after him, calling frantically.

"I ain't gonna wait!" shouted the ferryman.

Judge Anderson put his pistol on the seat beside him. "Every boy's dog is important. You can very well wait. If this is your last trip, what difference does five minutes make?"

There they stayed until Chubby returned, muddy and breathless with Kentucky tied to a strip of rawhide. The judge put away his pistol and allowed the ferryman to cast off. Page, Marker, and Red rode their horses aboard and dismounted to help pole the raft across as the angry Brazos swirled around their feet.

It took all three of them to pull the wagon through the mud of the east bank and onto the now well worn trail to Nacogdoches. Red Regan started to dismount. "I'll tie your horse back of the wagon, Judge."

Judge Anderson looked at the redheaded boy the village had ignored. "You take the sorrel, Red," he said. "I won't have need of it."

Red Regan looked up warily. "I might not bring your horse back. Animals get killed, you know."

"We can afford to lose horses, son, but remember, we can't afford to lose any men from Serena. Good luck!"

Red sat tall in the saddle. "Thank you, sir."

It was the first time Page had ever heard Red Regan say "sir" to anyone.

The wagons were moving out now. There was no time for tears or long farewells. Page kissed his mother goodby and watched the long line of refugees roll on to safety.

Then with Red and Marker he turned his horse south toward Sam Houston's army on the east bank of the Brazos. He had completely forgotten that today was his sixteenth birthday.

CHAPTER TWELVE

The Ragged Army

For two days, Page, Marker and Red camped on the east bank and watched Sam Houston's army move across the flooding Brazos on the sturdy steamboat *Yellowstone*.

As straining oxen pulled the last of the heavy wagons up the steep bank, the blacksmith decided it was time to ride into camp and join up. Page felt excited and proud as they trotted through the drizzle of rain to Donahoe's plantation where the army had encamped. He could almost see himself being sworn in by a handsome, uniformed officer in a tent where aides rushed to and fro on official business.

But no such place existed except in the history books Page had read. There was no headquarters tent. There were no tents at all. There were no uniforms. The unkempt men who squatted around cooking fires wore mudcaked buckskins. They were haggard and tired and short of speech.

Over and over Marker inquired, "Howdy, where do we join up?" No one seemed to know or care. Finally, at the edge of the circle of fires, they came on an old man drinking his coffee alone.

"Where's the place to join up, sir?" Page asked.

The old man looked up eagerly. "Well, light and set, boys. I don't reckon no one can sign you up afore sunup. Things is just about as snarled up as they can be in this army. Get recruits and lose deserters. Here, have some coffee."

Marker accepted the invitation. "Might as well give up and get some rest, boys. Stake out the horses, Red. You break out some grub, Page."

While they ate, the old man talked. "Me, I sorta latched onto the army back there at Gonzales. Bet I'm the oldest man in the company. Old Bailey, that's me. Kept telling me to go on with the women and children in the wagons. But I aim to fight."

Page watched the leathery brown face in the firelight. "You could still go to Nacogdoches, sir."

Bailey ran a finger over his well polished rifle. "I ain't so old I can't see right down this barrel. Comanches got my son. The Mexicans burned my house. I got a score to settle. I'm sticking with Sam Houston."

Red Regan took a piece of beef off the fire. "I hear tell mebbe Sam Houston don't never mean to fight at all."

Old Bailey's eyes narrowed in anger. "Hold your

tongue, boy. I been on this march now for three weeks—
mud, rain, cold, no rations, just slogging along one
durned sloppy mile after another. Sure, we been retreating, clear from the Colorado river right across the Brazos.
But mark my words, boy, Sam Houston has a plan. Don't
ever let me hear you throw off on him again like he was
yellow and running from a fight!"

The blacksmith tried to make amends for Red's re-
mark. "Like as not, Mr. Bailey, you're right. Sam Houston
isn't just retreating. I think he is drawing Santa Anna
into a trap."

The old man prepared to roll up in his poncho. "Well,
the Gin'ral, he don't tell anyone his plans, not even his
officers. He just keeps it to hisself. That's why the talk
is there will be another Gin'ral if he don't haul off and
fight before long."

Page shucked off his boots. "Sure are a lot of rumors.
I heard one soldier say we'd move out at daybreak, and
when we come to the fork in the road, that will tell the
story."

"You mean Houston can take the road to Nacogdoches
and run out of Texas or turn south and catch up with
Santa Anna?" Red said wryly.

Old Bailey put his battered hat over his eyes. "I tell
you Sam Houston ain't about to run out of Texas. Took
in a Mexican yesterday and found out Santa Anna and
his army couldn't cross the Brazos at San Felipe. They
had to go down to Harrisburg to get across. That means

we're both on the east bank of the river now and there's going to be some fighting afore you know it."

The next morning, Old Bailey took them to what passed for headquarters and Marker proudly signed his name to the roster. Without asking, he also signed Red's name and let him make an X after it. Red's face flushed as he watched Page sign in a fine flowing hand.

Assigned to a rifle company, they watched the uneven columns of men move out into the never-ending rain. As he fell in, Page couldn't be comfortable in the saddle with Old Bailey walking in the mud. But before he could dismount, Red grabbed the old man roughly by the shoulder. "Here, you take my horse. I'm a good walker."

That's the way the march went. Old Bailey rode the sorrel and Page and Red took turns walking in the downpour that slowed the army to a scant sixteen miles by dusk.

Now the three recruits looked like the rest of Sam Houston's ragged army. They had spent the day pulling wagons out of the mire. They were tired and muddy and hungry. Camp was made one mile short of the crossroads where the decision would be known.

Before they had a chance to build a fire, an officer came riding through the camp asking for a blacksmith. Marker sighed and took out some cold jerky. "I guess that's me, boys. You stick together and take care of Old Bailey." He rode off toward the supply wagons where a

forge had been set up and horses were waiting to be shod.

Old Bailey fed his fire carefully with dry twigs. "Guess they need Wilson to cut up nails and horseshoes for ammunition."

"Ammunition for what!" jeered Red.

"Ain't you seen the Twin Sisters? Those two six pounder cannon was sent clear west from Cincinnati, Ohio, by friends who think Sam Houston knows how to use them. How do you like that, Mr. Know-it-All?"

One of the company officers paused before their fire and looked carefully at the three of them—an old man of seventy, a tall thin boy, and a heavy shouldered, sullen faced youngster of fifteen.

"You're new. What did you do before you joined up?"

Red Regan grinned. "Farmer. Strong enough to pick cotton from sunup to sundown!"

The man smiled at his bragging. "In that case, you won't have to have a horse. We need it. Here, sign this requisition paper."

Red's swagger left him. Meekly he made his mark.

"You there, what can you do?" the officer asked Page.

"Innkeeper and schoolmaster, sir." He heard the officer laugh. He heard Red Regan join in. "I can walk any distance you name. Take my horse if you have need of it. But Mr. Bailey, here, is not so young. He needs a horse."

Old Bailey flapped his arms like a banty rooster. "I

· 160 ·

don't need any of your horses. I kin walk as good as the next man."

The lieutenant sized him up. "I guess you'll have to, or else ride one of the wagons. Cavalary is short on horses."

Red Regan brought up the sorrel with Charcoal and handed the reins to the lieutenant.

Page wanted to tell the little black mare goodby, but this was the army. He said nothing.

"Now you three," the lieutenant ordered, "will take rear guard duty tonight. See anything suspicious, report at once."

"Just when I had my fire started," Bailey grumbled, picking up his gear. "Come on, you two young'uns. I'll stay awake longer than either of you."

But Old Bailey didn't stay awake. It was Red Regan who took his watch for him and never wakened the old man.

As they joined the last column out in the still falling rain the next morning they could feel the excitement mounting as the army neared the crossroad. Would Houston turn north to safety or south to meet Santa Anna?

Then a sudden cheer rippled down the columns. Men yelled and capered and clapped each other on the back. Sam Houston had turned south toward Harrisburg, riding at the head of his army on a mud-splashed white horse.

"What did I tell ya," gloated Old Bailey. "Sam Houston ain't running out on no fight!"

Red said nothing, but when Old Bailey mired down in the mud a mile further out on the prairie, young Regan picked him up and toted him to drier ground. "After this," he ordered gruffly, "climb on my back before I have to dig you outa this quagmire. You want to fight so bad I'll see you get there, Bailey!"

The old man chortled from Red's shoulders. "Page, this here boy don't mean half he says. Sure wish I had me a juice harp or something to make music."

Page fumbled in his pack and came up with the fife. Heads turned and steps lightened as the shrill notes echoed down the road. He played "Come to the Bower," for it was the only song he knew. It wasn't exactly marching music, but to the tramp of feet he quickened the tempo.

A soldier in front of him began to sing. Others joined in.

Will you come to the bower I have shaded for you?
I have decked it with roses all spangled with dew.
Will you, will you, will you
Come to the bower?
Will you, will you, will you
Come to the bower?

The men's spirits rose and good humor returned. They knew they were no longer being chased by Santa

Anna. They were pursuing the Mexican general now, right down the east bank of the Brazos.

The rain ceased and an almost forgotten sun rolled into the cloud-streaked sky. The bluebonnets and Indian paint brush formed blue and crimson lakes on the emerald green of the prairies. A rabbit scuttled into the brush. A mockingbird sang from the scrub oak. Page looked at the sudden beauty of Texas in April and could scarcely believe he was marching to war.

Around the campfires at night there were tall tales and cheerful talk, but for Page, Red, and Old Bailey, on guard duty, the evenings were long and quiet. There was danger of all of them going to sleep.

Page wondered what he could do to keep the old man awake. First they played checkers with stones on a square drawn in the soft earth. When they had finished, Page tallied up wins and losses and signed his name with the stick.

Old Bailey watched with envy. "Sure do wish I could write my name real purty like that!"

"Why not?" Page asked. "I could teach you in no time. What's your first name?"

The old man shook his head. "Long time ago I had one, but I been Old Bailey so long, nary a soul would know who Robert Bailey was. Let's just learn me to write 'O. Bailey'."

Carefully Page scraped the ground smooth and with a sharp stick printed the letters. "Now, you copy those letters and in no time you can put them together in writing. Make three copies before I come on watch."

"You can't fight a war by writing letters!" Red snapped.

"No, but I aim to learn to write before we get started fighting. Why don't you try too, Red?"

But Red went back to his blanket without bothering to answer.

In two and a half days, the Texans marched fifty-five miles. They knew they were on the trail of an army that gave no quarter. Harrisburg was in ashes. Nothing had been left along the way.

The men were no longer tired. They were taut and tough and ready to fight. Santa Anna was only ten miles away, according to the scouts. When and where would Houston fight?

Page didn't know. Trailing the army as rear guard, he had never seen General Houston. He hadn't even seen Marker Wilson since the march started. But he wished he could find the blacksmith, for the lock on his old gun needed fixing again.

The army came to Buffalo Bayou and Houston put his men across on a floor torn from a log cabin. It was a slow raft but a steady one.

Word was passed down the lines to close ranks. Wagon wheels and gun mounts were muffled in rags and the army moved silently eastward to the grove of oaks that stood to the left of the bayou.

They crossed a narrow span, Vince's Bridge, over another bayou. "Mark my words," whispered Old Bailey, "the Gin'ral will send someone back to stomp down that bridge. That means we ain't got no way to escape. We're gonna fight it out!"

Page looked off across the prairie. He knew that beyond that rolling plain lay the army of Santa Anna, twelve hundred strong. Night laid down a black curtain, but still Houston's men crept slowly forward until they were almost at the junction of the San Jacinto River and Buffalo Bayou.

Then came the welcome order to halt and disperse in the grove. Quietly the men bedded down with cold rations and thoughts of tomorrow.

Old Bailey looked up at the moonless sky. "Too dark for a writin' lesson, Page. Don't matter, though, cause I can do real good. We got to sign that roster again tomorrow, don't forget."

Page didn't remember the faulty lock on his rifle until he heard the guard change in the early dawn. Quickly he pulled on his boots and set off with his gun to find Marker. He looked at many sleeping men, but none of them was the smith from Serena.

Then at the very edge of the grove he saw a forge set up and a towering man in blackened buckskins working the bellows. "My rifle has need of repair, sir. I think it is the lock. Could you fix it?"

The big man paused in his work. "Set it down, son. Call around in an hour."

Page hurried back to Old Bailey to get his share of the fresh beef ration, washed down with strong coffee.

The rest of the camp was just beginning to stir when Page judged by the sun an hour must have passed. He was anxious to get his rifle back. No telling when the attack would come.

He almost ran back to the forge where he had left his gun with a blacksmith he had never seen before. The rifle was ready and waiting. "Thank you, sir," Page said.

"Any time, boy. You'll have need of that rifle. Use it well!"

As Page walked away, he saw Marker Wilson striding toward him. "Want that gun fixed, Page?"

"I couldn't find you anywhere, Marker, so that smith up there repaired it."

Marker's mouth dropped open. "You asked *him* to fix your gun!"

"He was the only blacksmith I could find."

Marker shook his big head in wonder.

"But he's a blacksmith," Page protested.

"Land almighty, boy, that's General Sam Houston!"

Page turned back to offer his apologies to the General, but there was no time. The sharp notes of a bugle drifted across the prairie from the Mexican camp. "To arms! Stay in the woods!" Houston roared.

Page ran back to his own campfire. Santa Anna was ready to attack.

CHAPTER THIRTEEN

The Battle of San Jacinto

"Bet we was the only ones got to eat our breakfast!" Old Bailey gloated, as he joined Red and Page in the rear rank where they had been assigned. He looked around at the half-cooked meat and overturned coffee mugs. "Sure is a waste of prime coffee."

"Fine time to think about coffee in the middle of a battle," Red grumbled.

"This ain't no real battle," Old Bailey pointed out calmly. "This here is just a feeler from old Santa Anna, so don't get in such a swivet."

Page wondered. Across the prairie from the Mexican camp came a line of skirmishers backed by a column of infantry, and another of cavalry. They hauled a twelve pound cannon between them.

The Twin Sisters, already set up at the edge of the

grove, were primed and ready to fire. Houston, riding back and forth in front of his men, gave the signal. The Texas cannon roared, tearing away the carriage of the Mexican field piece.

The Mexican gun replied, but the aim was bad. Only green leaves and twigs showered down on the Texans in the grove. The first line of Mexican infantry advanced and fired, wounding one Texas officer and nicking the bridle of Houston's horse.

The men in the grove waited with trigger fingers tense. Houston's voice rang through the trees: "Fire!" The line of Mexican skirmishers sagged into the grass. The Twin Sisters spoke again. The shattered Mexican cannon was abandoned and the companies of Santa Anna retreated.

Old Bailey had been right. The Mexican general was not yet ready for a full scale attack.

"Our turn never came to fire," Red complained. "Why don't Houston fight now while they're on the run?"

Page heard many men asking the same thing as they drifted back to their breakfast fires. Old Bailey put his rifle down and rested his back against an oak tree. "You're just like a lot of other hotheads, Red. If Gin'ral Houston had a fought ever time some of his men wanted to cut loose on the Mexicans, there wouldn't be no Texas army now. You'll get your bellyful of fighting, so don't be in such a danged hurry."

"You think Houston can do anything, don't you?" Red taunted the old man.

Page tried to end the argument. "I found out he can do more than lead an army. See this rifle? Sam Houston fixed the lock himself." Page told, then, how he had mistaken the general for a blacksmith.

Red's laugh was mean. "Just like a schoolmaster not to know a general from a smith!"

Page flushed with embarrassment. Old Bailey quit whittling and stuck his Bowie knife in the ground. "Red, you remember a few days back when you was helping to lift a wagon outa the mud and they was a big man on the other side lifting too?"

"Sure, what about it?" Red demanded.

"Seems like you told him to get his back into it and do his share, didn't you?"

"I don't aim to do another man's work," Red blustered.

The old man took up his whittling again. "Just thought you might like to know that man was Gin'ral Houston. He knowed you was a raw recruit and never dressed you down. It ain't just a schoolmaster can't tell a gin'ral from his men in this army, boy."

For the first time, Page saw a shamed look in Red Regan's eyes.

Old Bailey's face softened. "Red, it's time you learned not to throw off on everybody. If a gin'ral can learn to hold his tongue, seems like you could do the same."

The morning passed and the afternoon dragged on.

The men were taut and ready. They had smelled powder. Page cleaned his gun and examined his knife for the third time. Red paced restlessly around the oak tree. Only Bailey stretched himself out for a nap. "At my age," he said, "it don't make no difference whether I fight today or tomorrow. Now quit tramping around, both of you, and let a man get some rest."

Finally, Page could no longer stand the waiting. He reported to the nearest smithy and helped break up nails, horseshoes and scrap iron into ammunition for the Twin Sisters.

Night came and still no sign of action from the Mexican camp. Nor was there word from Sam Houston except "Post guards and turn in." Red and Old Bailey rolled in their blankets and were still.

Page sat by the dying fire and looked out over the "Plain of St. Hyacinth." He could see that the Texas army lay with its back to Buffalo Bayou. On its left was the San Jacinto River, on its right Vince's Bayou. And before it, across the low prairie, was Santa Anna.

Old Bailey had been right in his surmise that Houston would have Vince's Bridge cut. With that link destroyed, there was no way out for either army. It would be a fight to the finish.

Surely, Page thought, the attack would come in the early dawn. He wished he knew who was riding Charcoal. He wondered if his mother had reached Nacogdoches. Had Serena been put to the torch, like other Texas towns that lay in Santa Anna's path?

But his mind kept coming back to the battle ahead. Could he bring himself to kill? Would the knife sing as Jim Bowie said it would? He knew he was no crack shot. What if he missed?

He was so engrossed in his thoughts he did not hear Old Bailey sit down beside him in the darkness. "You thinking on the fighting, boy?"

Page could barely see the wise old face in the dim light of the embers. "Yes," he said honestly. "I guess I am afraid. Afraid I can't do what is expected of me."

"Nothing to be ashamed of, son. Anyone says he ain't a mite afraid afore a battle starts is a fair to middlin' liar. I was scairt at King's Mountain fighting the British. And I was scairt fighting my first Comanches. I'm scairt now, afeared I might be too old to wrassle one of these Mexicans down, come hand to hand fighting."

"Jim Bowie once told me there comes a time when a man has to fight," Page said. "And my grandfather who was at Valley Forge always said that freedom was a hard bought thing."

"Them two men, was both right, son, God rest their souls. But just remember, that when the shooting really starts, you get so busy you plumb forget about being scairt. You bed down now. Like as not we'll be fighting before breakfast. The Gin'ral, he don't care whether a man gets his coffee or not!"

But morning reveille at four o'clock was the same as usual—three taps on a drum. There was no grumbling this day. Every man looked to his rifle priming, tested the keen edge of his Bowie knife, and waited.

The sun touched the grove now. Still no order came for an attack. The soldiers talked among themselves. What was Houston waiting for? Then they saw a long column of men march into Santa Anna's camp.

"Reinforcements," Red muttered.

"Between three and four hundred," Page agreed.

"Wonder what the Gin'ral's waiting for?" Old Bailey voiced a question about Sam Houston for the first time.

The sun climbed higher and the men became restless. They were too wary to relax and eat. But still Sam Houston gave out no hint of his plans.

At three o'clock, a young officer came hurrying through the camp, questioning one man, then another, until he came to the oak tree where Old Bailey napped with his hat over his eyes while Page and Red polished their already spotless rifles.

"Which of you has the fife?" he inquired.

"I do," Page answered.

"Compliments of the General. He would like for you to pipe the men into battle when we attack."

"Thank you, sir, but I can only play one tune. 'Come to the Bower' is not a marching song," Page protested.

"It will have to be," the officer said briskly. "General Houston heard you playing after we turned off to Harrisburg. We have no other instrument in camp. When the order comes, place yourself between the second and third line of troops and strike up your tune."

"Yes, sir," Page said. I've come to fight a war, he thought, and now they want me to play a fife. Perhaps they know I'm not a good shot. His spirits drooped as he watched the officer waken Old Bailey.

"Can you beat a drum, old man?"

"Never beat a drum in my life."

The lieutenant would have gone on, but Red Regan stopped him. "I can beat a drum. Want I should go with the fifer?"

The officer looked relieved. "Yes, I'll send down the drum."

Page turned in amazement. "I never knew you were a drummer."

"I never really had no drum," Red said slowly, "but I always wanted one when I was a young'un. Used to practise on a hollow stump with corn stalk sticks. Besides," he added, "no call for you to go out there tooting a fife by yourself."

Old Bailey reached into his shirt and pulled out a rumpled parcel. "Ain't neither of you going alone. I'm marching with you and acarryin' this flag." He unrolled the package and shook out a wrinkled square of white marked red and blue with a slightly crooked star. "My wife, Martha, made this here flag and I toted it clear from Gonzales. Surprise for the Gin'ral!"

Page saw Red swallow before he spoke. "That's a good flag, Bailey. Here, we'll fasten it to this stick and you march between us."

They attached the mud-flecked flag to a sapling. A messenger delivered the drum and Page took out his fife. Slinging their rifles on their backs, the three of them watched and waited .

The camp was still in the warm drowsy sunlight, tight as a fiddle string, strained as a tow rope.

Suddenly, the sharp call to arms shattered the silence. "Form ranks!"

Now all at once the camp was alive. Saddles creaked, horses reared, officers shouted. As Page worked his way through the first two lines and took up his position with Red and Old Bailey, he caught a glimpse of Marker Wilson in the first line of troops. He could see Sam Houston riding back and forth on the white stallion.

On the left, the first and second infantry regiments formed. The two cannons were in the middle, flanked on the right by the regulars and the cavalry.

Page did not have to be told the odds. He knew the Texan army numbered seven hundred and eighty-three men. Santa Anna had at least fifteen hundred.

"I told you the Gin'ral was smart," Old Bailey whispered. "Them Mexicans is sound asleep, taking a siesta!"

Red grinned, "Get them with their boots off, I bet!"

"When can we quit playing and start shooting?" Page asked.

Old Bailey pointed through the ranks to the five foot barricade of saddles in front of the Mexican camp across the plain. "Just afore we get there, throw down your fife and drum. I'm aimin' to get to that flagpole if I can duck enough bullets."

Red nodded to Page over Bailey's head. "We'll keep you covered, Bailey!"

Word was passed down the line. "Play!"

Page lifted his fife.

> *Will you come to the bower*
> *I have shaded for you?*
> *I have decked it with roses,*
> *All spangled with dew.*

Heads lifted. Feet tapped the time. Red joined the fife with a quick ruffle of the drum.

Sam Houston raised his sword and led the advance. The cavalry moved out quickly. The two six-pound cannons bounced through the lush green grass. The infantry pushed on, their rifles at the ready. Someone shouted, "Victory or death. Remember the Alamo!"

The cry spread through the ranks like a prairie fire.

Steadily the Texas lines approached the Mexican barricade of saddles. At twenty yards, Houston turned his horse and waved his hat. At that signal, the gun crew wheeled the cannons around and pointed them toward the barricade. With a roar, the Twin Sisters hurled a

charge of horse shoes, scrap iron and nails into the Mexican defenses.

Page threw down his fife and seized his gun. He heard Houston's cry, "Remember the Alamo, remember Goliad!" Almost to the barricade, the first line paused and sighted down their long barrels. A sheet of flame leaped across the breastworks, mowing down scores of grey-clad Mexicans.

The first line was over the barricade now, using clubbed muskets to knock the pistols out of Mexican hands. Over went the second line, wielding knives against bayonets. Horses reared and screamed. Metal struck against metal, wood smashed heavily into skulls.

The Mexicans, caught by surprise, were scattered, terrified, and confused. Soon the barricade rang with Mexican shouts, "Me no Alamo! Me no Goliad!" But because the Mexican army had killed without mercy, no quarter was given.

Page lost track of time and sound. He knew he had stopped, sighted and fired. He had climbed the barricade and whacked a man on the head with his rifle butt. He had fired his pistol. Now he pulled out his Bowie knife.

He saw men running on either side of him. He lost sight of Red Regan. In front of him loped the banty-legged little man with the Texas flag, straight toward the standard which held the Mexican banner.

Grey-clad figures streamed by, running in all directions. Some of them stopped to give battle with gun or bayonet. Others were unarmed. Bright-garbed cavalrymen rode for Vince's Bridge, not knowing it had been cut.

Page clutched his rifle and ran after Old Bailey, who was nearing the flagpole. The old man made it. Quickly he cut the rope with his knife and let the Mexican emblem fall to the ground. He was tearing his own flag from its stick and fastening it to the rope. Now he was raising the Texas banner.

Then, from out of nowhere, a shot tore through Bailey's leg and dropped him. Page looked up to see a Mexican running at him with a clubbed rifle. Swiftly he drew his knife. He heard it sing through the air and hit the target.

Someone back of him shouted. He turned as a shot rang out, and a Mexican loomed over him, closer, closer. He felt his head hit the ground. Something heavy fell across his chest. He glimpsed a man running toward him, a man with red hair. Then the sky rocked and wheeled. He knew no more.

CHAPTER FOURTEEN

Sam Houston Remembers

When Page opened his eyes again he could see the white-hot sunshine and blue sky. Something warm trickled over his hand. A weight on his chest made him breathe in short gasps. As his head cleared, he tried to raise himself from the ground, only to fall back in the dust.

Now he remembered. The battle. The flagpole where Old Bailey was fastening the rope after he had raised the Texas flag. Then the shot from a Mexican that tore through the old man's leg.

After that came the confusion of battle. The Mexican had run at him with a rifle. He remembered throwing the knife. He remembered a shout back of him, followed by a single shot, then a man with red hair running toward him as he fell.

Cautiously he raised his hand and tried to find his wound. Strange, he didn't feel any pain, only that weight on his chest. Then his hand encountered the braid of a uniform and a coat sleeve. Lifting his head slightly he could see a Mexican soldier lying lifeless across his own body.

Then the warm blood was not his own. Page almost laughed in relief. But where was Old Bailey? And where was Red Regan, who had shot the Mexican now sprawled across his chest?

Carefully he tried to twist and turn, but the Mexican was heavy and pinned him to the ground. "Bailey," he called softly. No one answered. He raised his voice. "Red, Red Regan!"

"Other side of the flagpole, Page. You all right?"

Page tried to keep the surprise from his voice at the first decent word he had ever heard from Red Regan. "Fine, here, Red, but I have a dead Mexican across me. I can't get up. How's Old Bailey?"

"I knocked him out so as he wouldn't suffer no more. He'll live."

Now, with the sun beating onto his face, Page suddenly wondered why Red didn't give him a hand. "Are you hurt, Red?"

"Got nicked by a bullet. Bleeding a little." His voice seemed to be fading.

"Look, Red, crawl over to me. I can use my hands. Take it slowly."

Page pulled at his shirt sleeve until it came apart. Then with his teeth he tore it again into strips.

After what seemed an eternity, he heard a body dragging through the gritty sand and saw Red Regan inching toward him. He heard the gasping breath as Red pulled himself on his belly, leaving a wet trail of blood behind him.

He knew Red was too weak to lift the heavy Mexican off his chest, but he had to get his head up to see better. "Red, shove your gun and gear under my head. Hurry."

With effort, Red did as he was told. Now, with his head propped up, Page could see what to do. He tore off Red's bloody shirt over a bullet hole in the limp arm. Quickly he bandaged the wound tightly, pulling until the spurting red stream stopped.

"Thanks," Red muttered and toppled over on his white face.

The sounds of battle seemed to grow fainter. Only a few scattered shots now. No more running feet. No more screaming horses. No more dull whacking of clubbed muskets.

Above him he could see the crude flag of Texas still whipping in the breeze. An almost eerie silence seemed to hang over the battlefield above the gunsmoke and dust.

He heard a man walking toward him. If his pants were Mexican grey, they were done for. But the feet were in moccasins. The breeches were homespun like his own. Page raised his hand and called for help.

"Land almighty, boy. Thought you was killed!" Marker Wilson raised the heavy Mexican body with one hand. Page scrambled to his feet.

"Not a scratch, Marker, but Red Regan got a ball through the arm. Lost too much blood. Old Bailey got it in the leg, but he's still alive. Can we get through the lines?"

Marker grinned. "Guess you lost track of things. Those Mexicans been whipped good. Took off across the plains or just give up. Battle's all over. Wish Jim Bowie could've seen it!"

Together, the blacksmith and the schoolmaster carried Red and Old Bailey across the littered battlefield to the oak grove where the wounded were being cared for by Doc Littlfield.

The Doc kept Old Bailey with the others, but turned Red over to Page. "He's young and healthy. Take him along, but watch his fever."

Red propped himself up against a tree trunk deep in the grove and slept while Page watched the battlefield below. Men were running here and there. Dead Mexicans were being buried. Guns were stacked, horses corralled. As the shadows of the trees grew longer Page dozed, only to be awakened by the feverish mutterings of Red. "I kin sign it. Two Rs and two Es and—"

Page bathed the hot face from his canteen and dribbled

water into the babbling mouth. Now he knew who had been making strange marks in the dust every night after he had given a writing lesson to Old Bailey. Red Regan. So he did want to learn after all. He was just too proud and ornery to say so!

Red at last slept quietly. When he awakened the grove was cool. His fever was gone. Page gave him some cold rations and filled his canteen. "Feel better?"

"Sure. Lick any Mexican regiment you name."

"Battle is all over. Texas won. Thanks for getting that Mexican who was about to shoot me in the back."

"Nothing to it. He was a sitting duck. Never knew you could throw a knife like that, Page."

"Jim Bowie taught me. Gave me a knife like his. I never killed a man before. Lucky throw, I guess. I can't repay you for saving my hide, Red. I'm not very good at building cabins or skinning buffalo or even chopping cotton. But I could teach you to write your own name in a few hours. Then you could sign the roster tomorrow and not have to make an X."

Red Regan kicked at the dust with his moccasins. "Can't. My right arm's hurt." But his face looked hopeful.

"Use your left hand. Lots of people do. Here, let me show you—" With his Bowie knife, Page started to print in the dust in large letters, R—E—D. "Now you do it."

Gritting his teeth against the pain in his arm, Red took the knife and awkwardly tried to copy the letters.

Over and over Page smoothed out the dust and Red

tried again, his mouth mumbling the letters and sweat rolling down his big face.

The light had almost gone when Page saw the weariness in Red's eyes. "We'll practice some more tomorrow."

Red's anger flared as of old. "I said I was gonna sign my name and I aim to do it. I ain't never backed out of a thing I set my hand to!"

"Not even making a schoolmaster's life miserable?"

"Give me that stick," Red demanded. "Now, show me how you join these here letters together so it looks like real writing and build us a cook fire so I can see."

Page finally dozed off with Red still humped over the dust with his knife, his teeth clenched, his eyes red-rimmed in the firelight.

When a bugle sounded, both of them reached for their guns and tried to stand up. Marker Wilson's laughter rang through the grove.

"That don't mean Mexicans a-coming! Sam Houston just got himself one of those fancy bugles to wake a body up. Old Bailey is better and hollering for rations. Red, you look like you'd make a hand except being a bit peaked. Get yourselves some breakfast and then come on down to that big tree. Everyone who fought the battle has got to sign the paper to get his share of land."

"What land?" Page asked.

"Sam Houston says everyone who fought yesterday gets six hundred and forty acres free and clear. Don't be late," he added, as he hurried on to rouse late sleepers.

"Land!" Red marveled. "I'll have some land for cotton of my own."

Page looked down at the ground beyond the dead ashes of their cook fire. There in perfect round letters in the dust was *RED REGAN*.

As they waited in the long line for their turn to sign the roster, little was said. The men were jubilant, but tired and anxious to be home. Page had signed his name opposite his signature on the list and started to turn away when he heard Red roaring in anger.

"It is *too* my signature. I kin write. I'll bash that face of yours into—"

Page caught Red's arm in time. "What's the matter, Lieutenant?"

The officer glared at Red. "That man signed his name a few days ago with an X. Now he signs Red Regan and expects me to believe he is the same person. Probably a deserter trying to collect on a battle he never fought."

Page felt the same cold anger he had known when he threw the knife. "Lieutenant, this *is* Red Regan. That *is* his signature. He fought in the battle. He saved my life."

"Then why didn't he sign his name in the first place?"

"Because he just learned to write his name."

"In the middle of a battle he learns to write!" the lieutenant sneered. "Get out, both of you."

From force of habit, Red tried to raise his right arm

to deliver a knockout blow. It was bandaged to his chest.

A ripple of laughter followed the two from the line.

Page kept a tight grip on Red. He could almost feel the hurt and humiliation settle over the boy at his side. He had felt the same thing himself too many times.

"Come on, we're going to see Sam Houston." After he had spoken, Page wondered if he had courage enough to do it. He knew Houston was wounded. He knew there were many things to claim the attention of a commanding general. But he could try. As Bowie said, sometimes a man don't know what he can do.

Silently they kept on walking until they reached the end of the grove where a circle of men stood watchfully over the man propped against a tree trunk. Page could see his battle weary face, his straggly beard, his powder-stained buckskins and bandaged leg. Houston scratched on a paper with a pen and handed it to a messenger.

Page straightened his shoulders and tried to break through the circle. A sentry tossed him roughly to one side. Red pushed the sentry back with his broad hand. "Here's a man who wants to see Sam Houston!" he bellowed.

Page caught a glimpse of the General looking toward the scuffle, and heard his tired voice. "If someone wants to see me, make a way for him, gentlemen."

The men fell back and Page pushed a now reluctant Red ahead of him. "Sir," Page began, "this man, Red

Regan, has been refused land on the grounds that he did not fight in the battle."

"Did he?" asked Houston gravely.

"He did, sir. He saved my life."

"Then what seems to be the trouble?"

"You see, sir, when he signed the roster several days ago, he could not write. He signed an X. That is no disgrace, General. Many of your best soldiers have never had the advantage of a schoolroom. But after he was wounded yesterday, he learned to write his name. The lieutenant will not believe it." Page paused, conscious of his torn shirt and bloodstained breeches.

Houston looked at him thoughtfully. "I recognize you now. You're the fifer. Where did you ever learn to play 'Come to the Bower'?"

"From my father, sir. Jefferson Carter of Virginia. He was a schoolmaster. He died on the way to Texas."

With an effort, Houston seemed to bring his mind back to the subject at hand. "I take your word for it, Mr. Carter, that your friend fought in the battle. But I can understand why the lieutenant was slow to believe a man could go to school and fight at the same time!"

Page found the Houston smile contagious. "After Red Regan got a bullet in his arm, I taught him to write his name. Kept his mind off the pain and fever, sir."

"You carry pen and ink with you, I presume?" Houston cocked an inquiring eyebrow at Page.

"There was no paper or pen, General. Red Regan

· 187 ·

learned to write his name with a Bowie knife in the dust of San Jacinto."

Houston pulled himself up straighter against the rough tree trunk. "Mr. Regan, I congratulate you as an apt pupil." He scratched on a bit of paper. "Here, take this to the lieutenant."

Page looked in admiration at the tall, gaunt figure he had followed for so many days. He could sense the full measure of the man, now. He was not afraid to speak. "Before the battle, I mistook you for a blacksmith and asked you to fix my gun. I am sorry, sir."

"Don't be. I am a very good blacksmith. You signed for your land, Carter?"

"Yes, sir. But I am not a farmer. I'm a schoolmaster at Serena on the Brazos. My school is just a cabin, but—"

The sentry at the edge of the circle guffawed loudly. "A schoolmaster and him only a mere boy! Who wants book learning to fight the Injuns and Mexicans?"

Houston's angry voice rolled like thunder. "You, out there, quiet!"

He turned back to Page who stood his ground, now without anger. "This is a rough frontier, Mr. Carter. A schoolmaster takes a lot of ridicule."

"I know, sir."

"I'll warrant you do. I know, too, because I was a schoolmaster once myself in Tennessee. I was only a few years older than you. It was not easy. But when I look back on it now—even though I have been governor and general—that year gave me the most satisfaction. I felt I was handing something valuable on from one generation to another."

Page for the first time in his life felt a glow of pride at being called a schoolmaster. He saw the Lone Star flag rippling in the wind beyond the General's head. The circle of men remained silent.

Houston extended his hand to Page Carter. "There will come a time in the new Republic of Texas when there will be more need for books than Bowie knives."

The sunshine lay over the land in a gentle haze as Marker, Red, and Page cantered down the familiar dusty road toward Serena. They had said goodby to Old Bailey. After searching the battlefield, they had found Page's fife. Their horses had been returned.

They had passed many stragglers. They had ridden through villages burned by Santa Anna and had seen homeless families drifting down the trails. Yet no one voiced the fear they all felt, that Serena would be only ashes.

Finally Marker put it into words. "Guess if Santa Anna burned the village, Page, you'll have to ride to Nacogdoches for your ma. You could take a stagecoach from there down to Galveston and stay until you get passage to New Orleans. 'Course if the Mexicans never got to Serena, your ma and all the rest of the folks will be back there by now."

Red Regan pushed his hat farther back on his head. "Reckon if you're pinched for cash, I could give you some of my land scrip. Not that it's worth very much."

Page tried to call back the picture of Virginia he had carried in his heart for so long—the brick houses, the white academy, the harpsichord in the parlor, the books on the shelves. But no, it no longer seemed real.

Instead he saw the rickety old ferry, the wagon-rutted main street, and the schoolroom with its rude benches and split log desks. He saw Old Bailey raising the home-made Texas flag. He saw Marker Wilson learning to write by candlelight. He saw Red Regan printing in the dust of San Jacinto. And he remembered Sam Houston's gaunt face.

"Thanks for the offer, Red. But I won't need any money. I'm not leaving."

Marker Wilson looked troubled. "But Page, if your school is burned, there's not a thing to keep you in Texas."

"If the school is burned, I'll rebuild it."

Red grinned at the smith, whose big face was beaming. "We'll all rebuild it, Page."

Marker seemed to have trouble with his throat. "We need you almighty bad, son."

They spurred their horses then and rounded the bend of the river, almost afraid to look. But Page could see that the town was still there, untouched and quiet in the sunlight. He knew now that he had come home.

CPSIA information can be obtained at www.ICGtesting.com
Printed in the USA
BVOW08s0609060615

403031BV00010BA/436/P